D0309422

THE
WEST
BROMWICH
ALBION
MISCELLANY

THE
WEST
BROMWICH
ALBION

MISCELLANY

DAVID CLAYTON

First published 2009

The History Press
The Mill, Brimscombe Port
Stroud, Gloucestershire, GL5 2QG
www.thehistorypress.co.uk

British Library Cataloguing in Publication Data.
A catalogue record for this book is available from the British Library.

ISBN 978 0 7524 5341 5
Typesetting and origination by The History Press
Printed in Great Britain

I'd like to dedicate this book to four people:

For Pete Wild (no 'e') – my best Baggies mate and a loyal (if somewhat displaced) fan of this most fine club

For Frank Skinner – entirely for *Fantasy Football*

To the memory of Laurie Cunningham

And the one and only Sir Bobby Robson

ACKNOWLEDGEMENTS

Thanks to Pete Wild for lending me his precious collection of Albion paraphernalia. To all the website editors and historians who may be unheralded in name, but I'd like to thank you for making all your hard work accessible for my research needs. A special mention to Tony Matthews (and Colin Mackenzie) for the superb 1987 collation of Albion history and stats and also to www.baggies.com for their boundless information. To Michelle Tilling, my editor at The History Press – this book arrived later than a Martin Jol tackle – and special thanks, as always, to my wife Sarah and our three beautiful young children, Harry, Jaime and Chrissie. That's pretty much it – for facts and figures from elsewhere, thanks as well. You know who you are.

David Clayton, 2009

A STROLL IN THE PARK

West Bromwich Albion Football Club actually began life (as if you didn't already know) as West Bromwich Strollers. In 1878, a group of men from Salter's Spring Works in West Bromwich decided to form a football team. With no club shop (there was no club yet!), no JJB Sports-type stores in existence and no Argos, the fledgling team needed the correct equipment, so after chipping in sixpence apiece, several of the prospective team took a stroll (you can see where this is leading) to neighbouring Wednesbury, several miles away, to buy their first football. Along the way, some bright spark suggested they should name their team after their excursion and so the club was christened the West Bromwich Strollers – though they are no relation to the San Francisco side, the Bay City Strollers.

BLOODY HELL

Who could ever forget the grisly clash of heads between Albion's John Wile and Ipswich Town's Brian Talbot which occurred during the 1978 FA Cup semi-final at Highbury? Well, Mrs Talbot and Mrs Wile for a start! Wile and Talbot emerged from a (literally) full-blooded challenge with gaping head wounds that would haunt the millions of TV viewers who were unlucky enough to watch it on *Match of the Day*. The memory of such heroics in the line of duty still remains strong in the minds of the Baggies fans who witnessed it more than 30 years on. Wile was Albion's Terry Butcher, a fearless warrior of the back four who spent 13 years as a player at The Hawthorns, clocking up 619 appearances in all competitions including exactly 500 in the League.

THE YAM-YAMS (THE WOLVES FANS): A DEFINITION

As per an official definition of a Yam-Yam, AKA supporter of Wolverhampton Wanderers: 'A person from the Black Country area of the West Midlands of England. Yam-yams use a slight variation of English that is often incomprehensible to non-locals (and even to their neighbours from Birmingham, with whom they share many similarities in vocal accent) due to both the thick accent of the speaker and the frequent exchange of standard words in place of local terminology. One of the most famous features is the 'yam yam' sound when saying certain phrases. 'You are' is pronounced 'yo'am' and 'are you' is pronounced 'am ya'.' So now you know – Bostin!

BAGGIES FANS RULE THE WORLD – OFFICIAL

In 2002/03, Albion's fans were voted the best in the Premier League by fellow Premier League supporters. Also in 2002, as part of the BBC's *Test the Nation* series, Albion fans were revealed as 'more likely to be smarter than any other football supporters, registering an average score of 138.'

BAGGIES ORIGINS

It's unclear when or how Albion acquired the nickname of the Baggies and it was a moniker the club initially used to frown upon. One theory is that it is derived from the heavy money-bags the gate men used to carry around the pitch perimeter in days gone by – or perhaps it was due to a baggy style kit the players once wore, but this seems unlikely as the kit the team played in was used for many years before the Baggies moniker started to do the rounds. Another suggestion is that the name was bestowed on Albion supporters by Aston Villa supporters, making a joke of the large baggy trousers (Madness, anyone?) that many Albion fans wore at work to protect themselves from molten iron in the factories and foundries of the Black Country. Of all the theories, however, it seems the gatekeeper idea may be the most likely of all nickname origins. When Albion moved to The Hawthorns in 1900, the club took the nickname of 'the Throstles' – a local name for the thrush, which was a common sight around the abundant hawthorn bushes the ground took its name from. The new ground had just two gates in its early years, one behind each goal, and on match days the gatekeepers would gather up the takings at each end and be escorted by police officers along the sides of the pitch to the centre line where a small office was located under the stand. The admission money, mostly in pennies, was carried in large cloth bags. It wasn't long before the gatekeepers' appearance in front of the main stand developed into a chant of 'here come the Baggies!' giving the team a new, if unofficial, nickname.

CREATURES FROM THE BLACK LAKE

The unknown, obscure and, as far as we can work out, now extinct tiny Midlands club Black Lake Victoria will forever hold a place in the history and, dare we suggest, hearts of Albion fans around the globe. It was Black

Lake Victoria who became West Bromwich Strollers' first official opponents on 13 December 1879. The game, played at Dartmouth Park, ended 1–0 to West Brom. The pioneers that day for the Baggies were: Biddlestone, Twist, H. Bell, T. Smith, Johnstone, Stanton, Bisseker (captain), Stokes, E.T. Smith, Timmins, Aston, and G. Bell. Around 500 people turned up and reliable sources suggest Harry Aston grabbed the winner. What became of Black Lake Victoria? Well, all we can find is this rather sorry piece of travel info:

'Black Lake tram stop is a tram stop in Black Lake in the West Midlands, England. It was opened on 31 May 1999 and is situated on Midland Metro Line 1. It is situated nearby the site of Swan Village railway station, which closed with the rest of the line in 1972.'

Next time you're passing that particular tram stop, give a moment's thought to the long-forgotten players of Black Lake Victoria – that could have been the Baggies!

CHINESE, JOHN?

Albion became the first British football team to tour China in May 1978 after the Chinese government approached the Football Association with the request of sending a decent team over with the intention of promoting the sport over there. Ron Atkinson's side played four matches on the tour, during which Baggies star John Trewick commented that he had no intention of going to visit the Great Wall of China because, as he so succinctly pointed out, 'If you've seen one wall, you've seen them all.'

Despite Trewick's reticence, the tour was an enormous success, attracting huge crowds, and was the subject of a TV documentary. A total of 239,900 fans watched the four tour games with more than 80,000 in attendance for two successive matches alone.

The historic tour results were:

Peking XI 1–3 Albion
A. Brown (2), Regis
Att: 80,000

China 0–2 Albion
Regis, A. Brown
Att: 89,400

Shanghai 0–2 Albion
Regis, Cunningham
Att: 40,000

Kwangtung Province 0–6 Albion
Regis (2), Wile, Martin, T. Brown, Cunningham
Att: 30,500

Ron Atkinson's side rounded the tour off with a game against a Hong Kong Select side, winning 3–0 with goals from Tony Brown, Regis and an own goal from Chi-Keung in front of an appreciative 18,000 fans.

PAID YOUR SUBS?

Substitutes were first introduced into the English game for the start of the 1965/66 season, though they were only permitted, initially, for injuries. Albion's first ever sub was Graham Lovett, who deputised for the injured Ken Foggo on 10 September 1965. Lovett was the

Baggies' first sub to play during an FA Cup tie too, three years later at Colchester United's Layer Road. He made a total of 15 appearances from the bench during his eight years at The Hawthorns (just in case you thought he spent his whole life gathering splinters).

AND I WOULD ROLL 500 MILES . . .

Here's a round-trip most clubs would have nightmares about – the Baggies travelled to London on 2 April 1926 to face Tottenham Hotspur at White Hart Lane, clocking up around 250 miles there and back. A day later they were away to Burnley – another 250-mile round trip, meaning they'd travelled about 500 miles in two days. Though Spurs won the first game 3–2, Albion showed plenty of spirit to win in Lancashire the next day 4–3.

MASCOT SCHMASCOT

There's only one bird any self-respecting Albion fan would be seen with on his arm – the club mascot Baggie Bird. OK, not the most exciting name in the world, but Baggie Bird does exactly what it says on the nest. He may be six foot tall and weigh more than Preston's Jon Parkin, but he's Albion through-and-through and cheep (geddit?) aside from being easily the best-loved mascot in England – not forgetting his offspring, Baggie Jnr, of course.

GET WITH THE PROGRAMME

The Baggies' first matchday programme debuted on 2 September 1905 for the home clash with Burnley. Entitled *Albion News*, it was eight pages long and cost one penny and it's fair to say if you've got one of the 2,000 that were printed for that match, it's worth considerably more today. Within two years the circulation had increased to 5,000, though it would be 69 years before the first colour matchday programme appeared in time for the 1974/75 campaign.

CLUB LEGEND: BOB TAYLOR

There really was only one Bob Taylor – a club legend who will go down in Albion folklore – but do you know all there is to know about Super Bob?

Name: Robert Taylor
Date of Birth: 3 February 1967
Place of Birth: Easington, County Durham
Position: Forward
Nickname: Super Bob
Early on he had unsuccessful trials for Newcastle and
    Hartlepool
1986: Began professional career with Billy Bremner's
    Leeds United
12/4/1986: Debut v. Millwall and went on to lose
    Division One play-off final to Charlton Athletic later
    that season
1988: Howard Wilkinson replaced Bremner as
    Leeds manager and Taylor finds himself surplus to
    requirements

March 1989: Moved to Bristol City with Carl Shutt moving in opposite direction

1989/90: Helped the Robins achieve promotion to Division Two and was named club player of the year, finishing as Division Three leading scorer with 27 League goals

January 1992: Signed for Albion for £300,000

1992/93 season: Finished as Division Two's top scorer with 30 League goals

1993: Promoted to Division One following play-off win over Port Vale

1993/94: League's top scorer with 18 goals but club struggled and only survived on the final day of the season

12/3/1996: Only hat-trick for club, v. Watford in 4–4 draw

1996: Scored 100th goal for Baggies v. Derby County – on the final day of the season

1998: A change of management and a struggle for fitness meant that Taylor was loaned out to Bolton Wanderers

A goal against Manchester United in his final game of a first loan spell gave him hero status among the Wanderers fans and was the main reason for his return for the final games of the season, though ultimately Bolton were relegated on goal difference

July 1998: Signed for Bolton for a fee of £90,000 where he played alongside Eidur Gudjohnsen

2000: Returned to The Hawthorns for a fee of £90,000 under management of Gary Megson. His goals kept Albion up that season

2000: His goal against Bolton in a 4–4 draw was voted the club's Goal of the Season

2001: Part of team that lost in the Division 1 play-offs to Bolton

28/10/2001: Became the 100th player to be sent off for WBA in a first team game when dismissed v. Barnsley

2001/02: Taylor's goals considered the main reason Albion are promoted to the Premiership

11/05/2003: Following an unsettled and inconsistent season, Taylor played his 377th and final appearance for WBA v. Newcastle United and received a standing ovation when he left the field after half an hour due to injury

13/05/2003: Taylor's testimonial match played at The Hawthorns

2003/04: Joined Cheltenham Town for a season

2004: Joined Tamworth

6/11/2004: Scored ten-minute hat-trick in the second half of a 3–2 win over Leigh RMI

2006: Joined Kidderminster Harriers

January 2007: Left Kidderminster and retired from football

HEAVEN SENT TALE

In March 2003, the following joke was knocking around various websites and was reproduced on Super Bob Taylor's official website – it pretty much sums up where SBT lies in the folklore of West Bromwich Albion Football Club . . .

Bob Taylor, Michael Owen and David Beckham are standing before God at the throne of heaven. God looks at them and says, 'Before granting you a place at my side, I must first ask you what you believe in.'

Addressing David Beckham first, he asks, 'What do you believe?' David looks God in the eye and states passionately, 'I believe football to be the food of life. Nothing else brings such unbridled joy to so many people, from the slums of Rio to the bright lights of Barcelona. I have devoted my life to bringing such joy to people who stood on the terraces supporting their club.'

God looks up and offers David the seat to his left. He then turns to Michael Owen. 'And you, Michael, what do you believe?'

Michael stands tall and proud. 'I believe courage, honour and passion are the fundamentals of life, and I've spent my whole playing career providing a living embodiment of these traits.'

God, moved by the passion of the speech, offers Michael the seat to his right.

Finally, he turns to Bob Taylor. 'And you, Mr Taylor, what do you believe?'

'I believe,' says Bob, 'that you're sitting in my seat.'

BIG RON QUOTES – VOLUME 1

Arguably Albion's most entertaining manager of modern times, Ron Atkinson is never short of a good line – or the occasional gaffe – here's the first of many. . . .

'Our fans have been branded with the same brush.'

Classic Ron

'The Spaniards have been reduced to aiming aimless balls into the box.'

Ron aims to please

'Liverpool are outnumbered numerically in midfield.'

As opposed to alphabetically . . . ?

'There are lots of balls dropping off people.'

Talking of dropping balls . . .

'The keeper should have saved that one, but he did.'

This sentence is an enigma wrapped in a mystery – a bit like Big Ron's 1980s comb over

'Their strength is their strength.'

Now he's talking . . .

'They are playing above the ground.'

This could have been in reference to a mining team

FROM RUSSIA WITH GLOVES

Albion became the first professional English football team to beat a Soviet side in their own backyard when they beat Dinamo Tbilisi 3–0 on 7 June 1957 thanks to goals from Horobin and Derek Kevan. Albion had already played Zenit St Petersburg five days earlier, drawing 1–1 in front of 80,000 people. The tour was completed with a 4–2 win over CDSA, the Russian Red Army side, again in front of a massive 80,500. Kevan scored twice to ensure he kept his record of scoring in every game.

BAGGIES SONGS – PART 1

Never let it be said that the Albion fans lack humour in the chants and songs that emanate from the terraces – here is a collection of classics, old and new:

(To the tune of 'Amarillo')
Is this the way to hammer Villa?
With lots of goals from Ishmael Miller
We'll be s***ting on the Villa
When Ishmael Miller scores for me.
La La La La La La La La
West Brom!
La La La La La La La La
West Brom!
La La La La La La La La
When Ishmael Miller scores for me.

(To the tune of 'Amazing Grace')
Boing Boing, Boing Boing, Boing Boing, Boing Boing
Boing Boing, Boing Boing, Ba-a-a-g-gies
Boing Boing, Boing Boing, Boing Boing, Boing Boing
Boing Boing, Boing Boing, Ba-a-a-g-gies
Go West Brom, Go West Brom!

Glory, glory West Bromwich,
Glory, glory West Bromwich,
Glory, glory West Bromwich,
And the Baggies keep marching
On, on, on!

Where's your job gone,
Where's your job gone,
Where's your job gone Rodney Marsh?
**Albion fans respond to the Baggies-bashing former
Sky Sports pundit's sacking**

(To the tune of Benny Hill's 'Ernie' – a superbly rewritten
ditty about Robert Earnshaw by Baggies fan Kevin Buckley)

You could hear the footbeats pound as he raced across the
  ground
And the clattering of defenders as they tried to bring him
  down
As he galloped onto balls to feet, his Throstle on his chest
His name was Earnie, could have been a better striker than
  the rest
Now Earnie's rightful partner, a bloke known as Kanu
Wore twenty five: it doesn't rhyme – Bernt Haas had 22
They said he was too good for us, a luxury player, chic
But he played Earnie in on goal a few times every week
Keep trying, Earnie
Earnie
He was more likely to score than all the rest (put together!)
His girl she wished to bathe in milk, he said, 'Right luv, for a
  larf'
And when he'd gone round hers one night, he filled a stand-up
  bath
He said, 'D'you want it pasteurised? 'Cause pasteurised is best'
She says, 'Earnie, won't you drown love, you only come up to
  my chest'
And they tickled old Earnie (well they would, she was a big
  girl)
Earnie
He was a quite a little short-arse – said in jest
Now Earnie had a rival, a quite good-looking man
Called Geoff Horsfield from Halifax, who once drove a
  brickie's van
He toiled away with his battling style and the balls aimed at
  his head
And when she seen the size of his tree-trunk thighs, well her
  cheeks turned very red. (As any girl's would, let's face it)

She nearly swooned when his shots ballooned but he said, 'If
    you feed me right

I'll win free kicks from defenders, though the goals scored will
    be tight'

He knew once she sampled his 'backing in', he'd have his
    wicked ways

And all Earnie had to offer was ten minutes some matchdays

Poor old Earnie

Earnie

But he was more likely to score than all the rest

The next match Geoff saw Earnie start a game we dare not
    draw

It drove Geoff mad with Earnie still not subbed at half-past
    four

And as he leapt down from the bench, hot blood through his
    veins did course

When he went to play him in first time, we'll he didn't half
    leave it short

No chance to pull the trigger

Trigger

Sandwiched by two centre-backs who came off best

So Earnie moved out into the space, and pointed with his hand

He said, 'If you want my place boyo, you'll score goals like a
    man'

'Oh why don't we win fouls for it?' Geoff sneeringly replied

'And just to make it interesting, we'll have AJ in the side!'

Now Earnie showed from gap to gap beneath the blazing sun

While Geoff stood with his back to goal, defender up his bum

But Earnie was too good, things didn't go the way Geoff
    planned

And a lovely Koumas through ball sent him goalwards past
    his man

(Tempo quickens even more [as it would with Koumas
    appearing!])

Then AJ gets between the ball and goal as Earnshaw shoots
And Earnie couldn't check his stride and the ricochet gets
   caught up underneath his boots
And he looks up in pained surprise as the goal he sure he's
   scored
Goes in off the arse of Horsfield, who had fallen on the floor
Earnie was only 23, it really made him sick
So now he's gone to make runs in a club where he's first pick
Where the midfield folk can pass it, and boots from the back
   are banned
And the forward's life is full of fun in that tippy, tappy land
But the Albion's needs were singlefold so they went with
   Geoff once more
But strange things happened right in front of goal, as he
   failed, each time, to score
Was that his own side shouting? Or the crowd that he could
   hear?
Or Earnie's ghostly image shouting 'Horsfield! Square it!
   Here!'?
They won't forget Earnie
Earnieeeeeeeeee
He was more likely to score than all the rest.

COMING TO AMERICA

During the summer of 1959, West Bromwich Albion
travelled to North America for an epic tour that took in
9 games in 20 days. Gruelling though the schedule was, it
turned out to be hugely enjoyable for the Baggies who won
seven, drew one and lost one, scoring 59 goals along the way
with Bobby Robson top-scoring with 12 and Ronnie Allen
one behind on 11. Here is the tour in full detail:

22 May: Ontario All Stars, Toronto, 6–1
Scorers: Whitehouse 2, Allen, Hogg, Robson 2
Att: 12,000

24 May: Dundee United, New York, 2–2
Scorers: Allen 2
Att: 21,312

27 May: Alberta All Stars, Calgary, 15–0
Scorers: Smith 3, Whitehouse 2, Kennedy, Robson 6,
G. Williams 2, Jackson
Att: 6,000

30 May: Dundee, Vancouver, 7–1
Scorers: Jackson 2, Kevan 2, Allen, Hamilton (og), Drury

1 June: British Columbia All Stars, Vancouver, 2–3
Scorers: Allen, Burnside
Att: 15,000

3 June: Manitoba All Stars, Winnipeg, 10–1
Scorers: Whitehouse 2, Allen 3, Robson 2, Kevan, Smith,
Kennedy
Att: 8,500

6 June: Dundee, Toronto, 4–2
Scorers: Allen, Burnside 3
Att: 10,000

8 June: Ottawa All Stars, Ottawa, 9–0
Scorers: Whitehouse 3, Burnside 2, Robson 2, Kevan,
Jackson
Att: 25,000

10 June: Montreal All Stars, Montreal, 4–0
Scorers: Allen 2, Hogg, Whitehouse
Att: 15,000

FA YOUTH CUP

West Brom first reached the prestigious FA Youth Cup final back in 1955, but came up against an exceptional Manchester United youth team – the Busby Babes, no less – and lost 7–1 on aggregate over two legs. United won their home leg 4–1 and the return at Albion 3–0. Incidentally, United had also ended the Baggies' interest in the competition the previous season, winning 7–1 on aggregate over the two semi-final legs! It was 14 years before Albion next appeared in the final, and though they gained revenge on Manchester United by dumping the Reds out at the semi-final stage, they lost to Sunderland 6–3 over two legs – this after taking a 3–0 first-leg lead! The Black Cats romped home 6–0 in the second leg after Asa Hartford and Jim Holton were controversially red–carded at Roker Park where just over 8,000 fans turned out with the tie seemingly all but over. In 1976, however, the Baggies finally landed the trophy with a particularly sweet 5–0 aggregate win over Wolves. Albion won the first leg at Molineux 2–0 and then finished the job at The Hawthorns 3–0 in front of 15,558 fans. Two years later Crystal Palace needed three semi-final matches to see off a talented Albion following two draws.

THE WATNEY CUP

Albion took part in the Watney Mann Invitation Cup – better known as the Watney Cup – on just one occasion. Though it was a short-lived pre-season tournament, there were a number of firsts that make it standout somewhat from the numerous other meaningless competitions that hold little or no interest with the paying public.

The Watney Cup was held in the early 1970s and was contested by the teams that had scored the most goals in each of the four divisions of England and not been promoted or admitted to one of the European competitions. Two teams from each division took part, making eight participants in total. The competition was a straight knockout format and each match was a one-off with no replays. Unlike most other competitions, the final took place at the home ground of one of the finalists, rather than a neutral venue. It was one of the first competitions in English football to be sponsored (Watney were a major brewery at the time) and Watney Cup matches were also televised live – a very rare occurrence in the 1970s. Running from 1970 to 1973, Albion's debut in the competition was in July 1971 away to Wrexham where two goals (including a penalty) from Tony Brown were scored in front of a decent crowd of 11,218. The Baggies then travelled to The Shay five days later to take on Halifax Town and, in front of 12,069 people, a Colin Suggett brace sent Albion into the final where they faced the might of Colchester United – job done, surely? The country's best cup side versus a struggling Fourth Division outfit who had beaten Luton Town and Carlisle United for the opportunity of taking on top-flight Albion at The Hawthorns – it should have been a canter. It wasn't, and despite 19,009 people turning up to watch the match, plucky Colchester just would not lie down and Jeff Astle's double plus Len Cantello and Suggett's goals were not enough to secure the Watney Cup for the hosts with the visitors matching them all the way in an entertaining 4–4 draw. As per the rules, the match went to penalties – the old lottery that levels most teams to gibbering wrecks, regardless of their division – and Colchester won 4–3.

FLOODS OF, ER, LIGHTS – AND GOALS

The Hawthorns installed floodlights at a time when most other English clubs were also constructing facilities that would enable night matches to be played, whether it be spotlights across the top of the main stands or, what would become the first thing most fans would recognise as a football ground from a distance, four huge metal pylons in each corner of the ground flooding the pitch with bright light. To celebrate the big switch on of the Baggies' lights, a prestigious friendly against the Russian Red Army (CDSA) was organised for 29 October 1957 to officially inaugurate the lights. Six weeks prior to this, Albion played their first night game against Chelsea on 18 September, drawing 1–1 in front of 36,835 curious supporters. The game with the Russians would have lit up any dull Midlands evening, with both sides committed to raw, entertaining football. With heavens opening and torrential rain falling throughout the game – which was covered live by BBC TV incidentally – Albion edged an 11-goal thriller 6–5, with goals from Kevan (2), Robson, Griffin, Allen (pen) and Howe sending the soggy fans home – 52,805 of them – in high spirits.

CHILES PLAY

Deadpan Adrian Chiles has recently taken the role of Albion's most prominent fan – here are a few memorable quotes from the popular *Match of the Day 2* anchorman and author of the excellent *We Don't Know What We're Doing*. . . .

'I live my whole life with the same feeling I have in my stomach when the Albion are winning 2–0 with half an hour left. In other words, it's all going terribly well, but it will still quite possibly end in misery.'

AC on a feeling all Baggies fans can relate to

'I love West Bromwich Albion. If West Brom are doing well, I'm good company. I'm a nice colleague, a good friend, a doting father, a loving husband. If, as is more often the case, we're doing badly, I am none of the above.'

Adrian on his split personality

'It's all about expectation really. I remember us going up to Old Trafford when we were in the Premier League and the United fans must have been looking at us thinking "How can you support a load of shite?" But the head of our supporters' club said one of our wins is worth 20 of theirs. Next week we beat Wigan 1–0 away and we were ecstatic, but how much would that mean to a United fan?'

Adrian, after being asked if supporting Man Utd would make his life easier

'A few years back I had a broken leg, and it was in plaster for seven months with my very crusty toes poking out of the end. An Albion fan came up to me in the pub and said, "Excuse me mate, but can I suck yow toe?"'

Adrian on 'unusual requests'

JUST THE 'TRICK

Remember Robbie Fowler's five-minute hat-trick for Liverpool against Arsenal some years back? We got that beat. W.G. Richardson cracked 3 goals in 3 minutes for Albion away to West Ham in 1931 – then scored again 2 minutes later to make it 4 in 5 minutes – the fastest quadruple, we reckon, in the history of football. Richardson was at it again two years later, though his 3 goals in 9 minutes against Derby County were scored at, shall we say, a more leisurely pace. Bobby Blood managed 3 in 5 minutes at Nottingham Forest in 1923 and Charlie Wilson managed 3 in 11 minutes against West Ham in 1924. Jimmy Cookson's incredible 38 goals from 38 League games during the 1927/28 season included 6 goals against Blackpool during a 6–1 win at The Hawthorns. The Manchester-born striker scored 110 goals in 131 appearances for the Baggies – a prolific record.

THE WHISTLEBLOWER

When Albion cracked in 13 goals during a friendly with Swansea in 1899, one shot from Billy Bassett deflected into the net off the referee, Mr T. Kinney, who was duly credited with the goal on the official scoresheet!

WOLVES AT THE DOOR

Black Country cousins and Albion-loving Wolves played two games at The Hawthorns in 1919 following unruly crowd disturbances at Molineux. The Football League granted Wolves permission to switch to Albion's home ground while the problems on their own patch were investigated. Wolves lost 4–2 to Barnsley and drew 2–2 against Stockport County during their two-game tenure.

CAN WE PLAY YOU EVERY WEEK?

Ask any Man City fan and they'll tell you the Baggies are a bogey team – to back that theory with facts, Albion's first League win at The Hawthorns was a 3–2 victory over City in October 1900, the record home win for the Albion was a 9–2 victory over City in 1957 and the Manchester Blues' heaviest home defeat? You guessed it – a 7–2 thrashing by the Baggies. The recent meetings between the clubs back up the Baggie Bogey yet further with 5 wins, 3 draws and just 2 defeats for the Albion in the last 10 matches from 2009 stretching back to 2001.

ENGLAND EXPECTS

England have played international matches on three occasions at The Hawthorns. The first match was on 21 October 1922 when England beat Ireland 2–0 in front of 20,173 fans with future Albion player Harry Chambers scoring both goals. Two years later, on 8 December 1924, England thrashed Belgium 4–0 with 2 each for Joe Bradford and Billy Walker in front of a meagre 15,405 fans. The only time England lost at The Hawthorns was on 20 October 1945 when Wales won 1–0, though the game, watched by 54,611 people, did generate record gate receipts of £8,573.

'I'M OFF TO THE MATCH, LOVE. SEE YOU IN A WEEK OR SO . . .'

And they think Premier League players have it bad today – well how about this? Postponements and an epic FA Cup run meant that Albion, in order to complete their League programme, had to play SEVEN games in TEN days from 20 April to 29 April 1912 – and two of those games were FA Cup finals! It's unthinkable today that teams play more than two games in a week, but imagine how cream-crackered the Baggies lads were at that point. Perhaps unsurprisingly, Albion failed to win one of the games and the League failed to take pity when they fielded what was, in effect, a reserve team against Everton on 22 April, even though it was sandwiched between the FA Cup final against Barnsley and the replay five days later. The Baggies were fined £150 as a result. Here's the 'mission impossible' the lads faced:

20 April	Barnsley	N	FA Cup final	0–0
22 April	Everton	A	League	0–3
24 April	Barnsley	N	FA Cup final Replay	0–1
25 April	Blackburn R	A	League	1–4
26 April	Bradford City	H	League	0–0
27 April	Sheffield W	H	League	1–5
29 April	Oldham Ath	H	League	0–0

TANNED IN BURNLEY

Albion's curtain-raiser to the 1906/07 campaign was played in heat registering 90 degrees in the shade at Burnley's Turf Moor, though it didn't prevent Buck's only goal of the game earning the Baggies a 1–0 win.

RECORD BREAKERS

Albion's record victory for a senior game came on 11 November 1882 when Coseley arrived hoping to pull off a shock Birmingham Senior Cup victory. By half time, their hopes were beginning to fade after the Baggies edged into a 17–0 lead. Coseley adopted a more defensive formation after the break and conceded just nine more to leave with a respectable 26–0 defeat. For the record's record, the goalscorers were Aston (5), Bisseker (4), Timmins (4), G. Bell (3), Bunn (2), E. Horton (2), While (2), Whitehouse (2), H. Bell and Stanton. Goalkeeper Roberts was the only player who didn't get on the scoresheet but in his proximity to the 2,500 people watching, he could hear moans on the way out that it 'should have been 27. . . .'

CHAMPIONS!

West Bromwich Albion Football Club might have only won the League Championship on one occasion, but there are only a select band of clubs who can claim to have achieved the feat. The Baggies' season of triumph was the 1919/20 campaign – the first since the First World War ended, giving the Albion fans the perfect pick-me-up after the conflict which had caused rationing and misery to millions of British people. Albion scored 104 goals and won 28 of their 42 fixtures to take the title and clinched the League on 10 April when nearly 30,000 fans saw West Brom beat Bradford City 3–1 at The Hawthorns. Here is the historic table:

1919/20

	P	W	D	L	F	A	W	D	L	F	A	Pts
1 West Brom	42	17	1	3	65	21	11	3	7	39	26	60
2 Burnley	42	13	5	3	43	27	8	4	9	22	32	51
3 Chelsea	42	15	3	3	33	10	7	2	12	23	41	49
4 Liverpool	42	12	5	4	35	18	7	5	9	24	26	48
5 Sunderland	42	17	2	2	45	16	5	2	14	27	43	48
6 Bolton W	42	11	3	7	35	29	8	6	7	37	36	47
7 Man City	42	14	5	2	52	27	4	4	13	19	35	45
8 Newcastle U	42	11	5	5	31	13	6	4	11	13	26	43
9 Aston Villa	42	11	3	7	49	36	7	3	11	26	37	42
10 Arsenal	42	11	5	5	32	21	4	7	10	24	37	42
11 Bradford PA	42	8	6	7	31	26	7	6	8	29	37	42
12 Man Utd	42	6	8	7	20	17	7	6	8	34	33	40
13 M'boro	42	10	5	6	35	23	5	5	11	26	42	40
14 Sheffield U	42	14	5	2	43	20	2	3	16	16	49	40
15 Bradford C	42	10	6	5	36	25	4	5	12	18	38	39
16 Everton	42	8	6	7	42	29	4	8	9	27	39	38
17 Oldham Ath	42	12	4	5	33	19	3	4	14	16	33	38
18 Derby Co	42	12	5	4	36	18	1	7	13	11	39	38
19 Preston NE	42	9	6	6	35	27	5	4	12	22	46	38
20 Blackburn R	42	11	4	6	48	30	2	7	12	16	47	37
21 Notts Co	42	9	8	4	39	25	3	4	14	17	49	36
22 Sheffield W	42	6	4	11	14	23	1	5	15	14	41	23

SLAIN BY MINNOWS – THE TRUTH

Ask any Albion supporter about the club's record since we last won the FA Cup – in 1967/68 – and they'll tell you that, more often than not, the Baggies have been dumped out by lower league opposition. In truth, there have only been a few cup upsets and Woking, Bournemouth, Swansea, Carlisle, Crewe, Plymouth and Leyton Orient apart, the list isn't that different from most other teams. The teams to knock Albion out are:

1968/69	Leicester City
1969/70	Sheffield Wednesday
1970/71	Ipswich Town
1971/72	Coventry City
1972/73	Leeds United
1973/74	Newcastle United
1974/75	Carlisle
1975/76	Southampton
1976/77	Manchester City
1977/78	Ipswich Town
1978/79	Southampton
1979/80	West Ham
1980/81	Middlesbrough
1981/82	QPR
1982/83	Tottenham Hotspur
1983/84	Plymouth Argyle
1984/85	Leyton Orient
1985/86	Sheffield Wednesday
1986/87	Swansea
1987/88	Wimbledon
1988/89	Everton
1989/90	Aston Villa
1990/91	Woking
1991/92	Leyton Orient
1992/93	West Ham
1993/94	Halifax
1994/95	Coventry City
1995/96	Crewe Alexandra
1996/97	Chelsea
1997/98	Aston Villa
1998/99	Bournemouth
1999/2000	Blackburn Rovers

2000/01	Derby County
2001/02	Fulham
2003/04	Nottingham Forest
2004/05	Tottenham Hotspur
2005/06	Reading
2006/07	Middlesbrough
2007/08	Portsmouth
2008/09	Burnley

LET THE MUSIC PLAY

Here is a selection of songs the Baggies have run out to at The Hawthorns in recent years. . . .

- 'Liquidator' by the Harry J. All-Stars – removed from the play list because of complaints that the chanting that went along with it was likely to provoke disturbances.
- 'Jump Around' by House of Pain – featured lyrics such as 'I never eat pork cos a pig is a cop' which went down well with the local constabulary!
- 'Oh Fortuna' from the opera *Carmina Burana* by Carl Orff – one of Denis Smith's last actions as manager was to suggest that the players' entrance onto the pitch should be inspired by something a bit more uplifting than had been used previously.
- 'Insomnia' by Faithless – mid-2000s
- 'Sandstorm' by Darude – mid-2000s
- 'Right Here, Right Now' by Fatboy Slim
- 'Lust for Life' by Iggy Pop
- 'Are you gonna be my girl' by Jet
- 'Pounding' by Doves
- 'Hate to say I told you so' by The Hives

COMMUNITY SPIRIT?

The Baggies have taken part in the FA Charity Shield (now known excitingly as the Community Shield) on four occasions. The first time was after winning the League in 1920 to take on Spurs at White Hart Lane and the Baggies left with a 2–0 victory to claim the shield for the first – and only – time, though they would share it for one season with Wolves. For the 1931/32 campaign, Albion lost 1–0 at Arsenal and the third Charity Shield encounter was at the start of the 1954/55 season when the Baggies and Wolves drew 4–4 to take the Shield for six months each. The worst occasion – and the last time Albion contested this traditional curtain-raiser in England – was in August 1968 when Albion, fresh from winning the FA Cup a few months earlier, took on Manchester City at Maine Road. More than 35,000 fans turned up to see City comprehensively thrash the Baggies 6–1.

The complete record for the Charity Shield is:
Pld:4   W:1   D:1   L:2   F:7   A:11

CELEBRITY BAGGIES

When it comes to celebrity supporters, the Albion have more than their fair share. Perhaps the most well-known is Frank Skinner, the stand-up comedian who shared his love of the club with the nation in the 1990s as a presenter of the cult TV show *Fantasy Football* along with David Baddiel. The pair then went on to record one of the most popular England records of all time with 'Three Lions'. Skinner gets to The Hawthorns whenever he can and once, when asked by a member of the audience how he felt now that Albion had been promoted to the Premiership, Frank thought for a minute and said 'Does the phrase "Dog with two dicks" mean anything. . . ?'

Another stand-up, Lenny Henry, has never hidden his love of the Baggies. Lenny used to be good friends with a lot of the players back in the days of Laurie Cunningham and Cyrille Regis. He has never been behind the door in his mickey-taking of Villa fans. During his Michael Jackson spoof 'Thriller' video there was a scene when he uttered the line, 'They look like they're fans of Aston Villa' with an accompanying shot of a group of zombies clutching claret and blue scarves. He often tries to squeeze a line in about being a Baggie into any TV work he takes on.

Britain's best-loved comedy actress, Julie Walters, is a huge fan of the Albion. She grew up in Cheshire Road, Smethwick, and her family still live there and when she is not working she will phone them to get tickets to watch her beloved Baggies play.

Other notable names include former *Who's Line Is It Anyway?* improv actress Josie Lawrence, former *Playschool* presenter Floella Benjamin and former *Coronation Street* heart-throb Matthew Marsden. Robin Asquith, star of the 1970s *Confessions of a . . .* movies is yet another comedic actor (though RADA trained!) who is continuing a worrying trend! The late Leslie Crowther of *The Price is Right* fame was a Baggies fan and Cat Deeley is another Baggie – despite coming from a family of Wolves fans. Legendary Hacienda DJ Dave Haslam is a Baggies fan, too. Dave wrote the book *Manchester, England* about the '80s rave scene up there. Rolling Stones bad boy Ronnie Wood was a boyhood Albion fan, Eric Clapton was rumoured to be a Baggie for a time and legendary ELO drummer Bev Bevan completes a notable trio of rock gods. Also, the majority of Judas Priest, two of the Fine Young Cannibals, members of The Beat and the drummer from The Charlatans make for an impressive musical representation. Tennis legends John McEnroe and Goran Ivanisevic are said to be honorary Baggies, while boxer Richie Woodhall is Albion through and through. Though there are loads more, *Match of the Day 2*'s Adrian Chiles has now taken over as the most recognisable and high-profile West Brom fan and he never misses a chance to tell the watching millions where his loyalties lie – as if it were ever in any doubt!

BAGGIES SONGS AND CHANTS – PART 2

(To the tune of Pigbag's 'Papa's Got a Brand New Pigbag')
La, la, la lah! Jason Koumas. . .
La, la, la lah! Jason Koumas. . .
La, la, la lah! Jason Koumas. . .

(To the tune 'There Were Three in Bed')
There were 11 on the field
And Warnock squealed: 'Fall over, fall over'
So they all fell over
and one was sent off

There were 10 on the field
And Warnock squealed: 'Fall over, fall over'
So they all fell over
And one was sent off

There were 9 on the field
And Warnock squealed: 'Fall over, fall over'
So they all fell over
And one was sent off

There were 8 on the field
And Warnock squealed: 'Fall over, fall over'
So they all fell over
And one was sent off

There were 7 on the field
And Warnock squealed: 'Fall over, fall over'
So they all fell over
And one was sent off

There were six on the field
And the Albion squealed:
'Neil Warnock
What a bleep
What a bleep
Neil Warnock is a . . . (use your imagination!)

(An ode to former Wolves and Villa boss Graham
Taylor)
Taylor is a turnip
He's got a turnip's head
He took the job at Villa
He must have been brain-dead
'Do I not like this?' and
'Do I not like that?'
But everyone in England knows
He is a . . . (use your imagination).

(To the tune of 'Would you like to swing on a star?')
Oh would you like to follow West Brom
Come up The Hawthorns and cheer 'em on
Remember Regis, Astle and Brown
Or would you rather be a clown?

A clown is an animal who follows the Blues
It sits on the Tilton just to watch its team lose

They've got no trophies
They've got no class . . .
[Rest deleted in case of lawsuits!]

Hark now hear,
The West Brom sing,
A king is born today,
And his name is Bobby Taylor,
And he's better than Stevie Bull!
Super, Super Bob,
Super, Super Bob,
Super, Super Bob,
Super Bobby Taylor!

The Lord's my shepherd,
I'll not want,
He makes me down to lie,
In pastures green,
He leadeth me,
The quiet waters by.

(To the tune of 'Go West')
Go West, Bromwich Albion
Go West, Bromwich Albion
Go West, Bromwich Albion
Go West, Bromwich Albion.

(To the tune of Boom, boom, boom!)
Say Boing, Boing, Boing, everybody say Baggies
BAGGIES!

THEY SAID WHAT? (AND WHY?)

'I think Darren would see most Championship clubs as a sideways step in his career but I don't think that would be the case with West Bromwich Albion.'

Peterborough's Barry Fry on rumours Darren Ferguson may be a managerial target for the Baggies

'He's done OK, but I thought last year was a wasted year, I really did. I honestly thought when they got promotion they'd consolidate, but there was a certain lack of experience.'

Big Ron on Tony Mowbray's departure

BAGGIES LEGEND – LAURIE CUNNINGHAM

He formed part of what was affectionately known as the 'Three Degrees' – an all-black American band who enjoyed enormous success in the UK during the 1970s – as did Albion's three black stars of the same era, Cyrille Regis, Brendan Batson and Laurie Cunningham. West Brom's talented trio arguably did more for black players in England than anyone else and the memory of that era evokes special memories in those who were lucky enough to witness it. Regis was powerful and direct; Batson was composed with a vein of steel while Cunningham was pure class.

The real crime is that this most talented winger should spend his peak years playing his football abroad, becoming the first Englishman to play for Real Madrid in the process – not bad for a kid who'd been rejected as a youngster by Arsenal and had to carve out a career instead at the more humble surrounds of Brisbane Road in the colours of Leyton Orient. After Cunningham destroyed Albion during an FA Cup tie, he quickly went to the top of Ron Atkinson's shopping list and Cunningham soon became a Baggies player and instantly struck up an understanding with Regis as Albion became one of the most feared teams in the top division.

'At that time, for a short spell I reckon we were the best team in Europe,' recalled former Baggies boss Atkinson. 'We didn't put any restrictions on Laurie – I just told him to get the ball at his feet and go and do damage with it. For that 1978/79 season, especially around the time when we beat Valencia in the UEFA Cup, I've never worked with a better player. I had Bryan Robson for years and at Atletico Madrid I had Paulo Futre, who was a European Footballer of the Year, but Laurie could live with any of those.'

While Cunningham and company blazed a trail, the racism at football matches steadily began to fade into the background as black footballers answered the bigots in the best way possible – by letting their feet do the talking. Cunningham became the first black player to be capped for England at any level, but it was a UEFA Cup tie against Valencia in December 1978 that changed his life forever.

'That was the game that everyone remembers,' recalled Cyrille Regis. 'He was electric; it was 90 minutes of sheer class. Everything went well – that performance captured whoever was looking for Real Madrid and sold him to the club.'

The deal to take this precocious talent to Spain took place at Ron Atkinson's house. 'We had our chairman Bert Millichip there and Madrid had their president there,' said Big Ron. 'They started bidding at £250,000 and we started at £1.5m – nobody spoke the same language except for the translator so we would write a figure on a piece of paper, show it to them and they would cross them out and put in their offer. That's how we did it. When they offered £250,000 my dog barked and I told them "look, even the dog knows that's not right."'

Both parties eventually agreed a fee of £950,000 and the 22-year-old Cunningham was on his way to the Bernabeu. 'It was a fantastic thing for him to achieve, to play for Real Madrid, but it was sad too because West Brom had a fantastic chemistry,' added Cyrille Regis. 'That was the start of their demise. Two or three years later Bryan Robson left, then Remi Moses did – I don't think the club has ever been the same.'

Injuries, however, took their toll and it was Big Ron who took Cunningham back to England during his spell as Manchester United manager. A loan deal was agreed but Cunningham couldn't win a permanent deal and returned to Spain before returning to play for Wimbledon and playing in the 1988 FA Cup final victory over Liverpool. He returned to Spain again to play for second division Rayo Vallecano and helped the team to promotion.

'I went out with him and the Vallecano president,' said Atkinson. 'He was saying how he was going to light up the Bernabeu next season and show Madrid what they had missed out on. A month or so later, he was dead.'

On 15 July 1989 Cunningham's life came to a sudden and tragic end in a car crash on the outskirts of Madrid.

'Laurie was like Cristiano Ronaldo in the way he used to take people on,' recalled Regis. 'He had his style, his grace and his pace. He ran on his toes, he was graceful with his amazing tricks and pace. I see him as never realising his potential. But talk to the second generation of black players who came after us, people like Ian Wright, and they will say when they saw people like Laurie on the pitch, they thought "if he can do that, then so can I."'

THE TATTERS

In the Black Country, the term 'Tatter' means someone who earns his/her living collecting and selling bits of copper, brass, lead, etc to scrap merchants and is one of the nicknames given by Albion fans to Wolves followers. As these items are usually acquired under somewhat dubious circumstances (i.e. a midnight 'visit' to local factories, for example) the term has come to mean someone who's little better than a common thief. The insinuation is clear for all to see and the estimation West Brom fans hold their Wolves counterparts in is slightly less than low. Well . . . you asked.

WHO PUT THE BOING IN THE BAGGIES? FAN THEORIES . . .

As with all good myths and urban legends, word of mouth and rumour are the most interesting source of information when trying to solve a puzzle – here are some theories taken from a West Brom fan site:

Theory 1: A local lad heard a record by a Dutch group called 'Poing!' and took such a shine to the tune and lyrics, he arranged to have it played in a local disco, where it caught on, accompanied by the jumping and flailing arm-movements we all know and love. This was subsequently imitated by the Brummie (at Orient of all places!) and it grew from there.

Theory 2: This peculiar mode of celebration was first unveiled as a charity fund-raising publicity stunt several seasons ago, at half time during a home game. It was called the 'Baggie Bounce' and various minor celebs took part, including the one and only Jeff Astle. The object of the exercise was to bounce up and down for a set period of time, at the expiry of which, a largish sum would be raised for charity.

Theory 3: The Albion were playing at Hull on a bitterly cold day. The travelling army, hoping to warm themselves up, started jumping up and down and shouting 'Come on you Baggies, Come on you Baggies,' in quick-time – and this was the birth of the Boing.

Theory 4: Boinging originates from an innocent remark made by reporter Malcolm Boyden in 1993 when he said 'the Baggies are boinging their way to promotion.' The Brummie Road took it up, and the rest is history.

THE GAFFERS

Jack Smith	1948–52
Jesse Carver	1952–3
Vic Buckingham	1953–9
Gordon Clark	1959–61
Archie Macauley	1961–3
Jimmy Hagan	1963–7
Alan Ashman	1967–71
Don Howe	1971–5
Johnny Giles	1975–7
Ronnie Allen	1977
Ron Atkinson	1978–81
Ronnie Allen	1981–2
Ron Wylie	1982–4
Johnny Giles	1984–5
Nobby Stiles	1985–6
Ron Saunders	1986–7
Ron Atkinson	1987–88

Brian Talbot	1988–91
Bobby Gould	1991–2
Ossie Ardiles	1992–3
Keith Burkinshaw	1993–4
Alan Buckley	1994–7
Ray Harford	1997
Denis Smith	1997–9
Brian Little	1999–2000
Gary Megson	2000–4
Bryan Robson	2004–6
Tony Mowbray	2006–9
Roberto Di Matteo	2009–

ALBION – FA CUP SPECIALISTS

West Brom's incredible record in the FA Cup has put them in the top ten all-time FA Cup league table, above the likes of Manchester City, Chelsea, Newcastle United and dozens of other notable clubs. Albion currently lie in eighth position with Blackburn and Spurs firmly in their sights. The table up to the start of the 2009/10 campaign is:

	Pld	W	D	L	F	A	GD
1 Man Utd	405	219	94	92	146	80	+282
2 Arsenal	408	214	98	96	149	85	+267
3 Everton	395	212	78	105	141	72	+271
4 Liverpool	398	209	90	99	168	102	+277
5 A Villa	395	204	79	112	113	78	+300
6 Spurs	379	191	95	93	118	70	+275
7 Blackburn R	383	187	84	112	123	82	+271
8 West Brom	372	181	80	111	115	78	+218
9 Chelsea	352	177	86	89	122	72	+230
10 Newcastle Utd	351	168	84	99	112	78	+182

ALBION – LEAGUE CUP

The Baggies are currently the nation's 20th most successful League Cup side, partly because they opted out for several years when the competition first began. Gallingly, Villa are the most successful League Cup side in terms of wins with 122, though Albion are comfortably higher than Wolves who lie in 29th position going into the 2009/10 season. The overall record is:

	Pld	W	D	L	F	A	GD
West Brom	153	68	37	48	243	204	+39

ALBION – ALL-TIME LEAGUE RECORD

The Baggies are currently England's 13th most successful club when all League games are totalled together from all 136 clubs who have taken part over the years – not a bad record, though [spit!] Wolves are fourth overall and Villa are seventh going into the 2009/10 campaign. A couple of good seasons and a couple of rotten ones for Sunderland, Bolton and Blackburn could see Albion move into the top ten and when the club tots up eight points during the 2009/10 campaign they will have earned a total of 5,000 points to date. The overall record is:

Home

W: 1130   D: 537   L: 548   F: 4150   A: 2592

Away

W: 581   D: 548   L: 1086   F: 2669   A: 3924

Pld: 4430   Pts: 4992   GD: 303

CREST AND A WAVE

Albion's club crest has undergone many changes over the past 130-odd years. The hawthorn image was not introduced until after the club's move to The Hawthorns stadium (why would it have done?) and originally the team crest comprised of a throstle placed upon a crossbar, the brainchild of former club secretary Tom Smith. During the early years of the club and up until as late as the 1930s, Albion were famous throughout the sport for placing a caged throstle pitchside as the senior side competed. Club myth claims that this throstle only sang when Albion were winning – it was a largely quiet bird and there were several occasions when it was suspected of suffering season-long laryngitis

Throughout the years, the club symbol has altered considerably, yet the throstle has been an ever-present fixture, with respect to the club's early nickname, the 'Throstles'. The club also paid tribute by constructing an effigy of the bird in 1979 and placing it above the stadium's half time scoreboard – if Albion were losing, they'd give the team the bird, so to speak. The crest continued to develop over the years with the white shield becoming a shield of blue and white stripes in homage to the traditional club colours.

Unlike many other clubs, Albion's team crest and strip badge have differed greatly over the years. Not until 2006 did the club register the crest as a trademark and for the majority of the Baggies' history a badge was not even incorporated into the team strip. The Stafford Knot took pride of place on the club's shirts in the 1880s, but not until 1960 did the club create an official badge. On the three occasions that Albion progressed to the FA Cup final, the club placed the West Bromwich town arms upon the shirt and in 1994 Albion integrated the club's motto 'Labor omnia vincit' or 'Work conquers all', though some have interpreted that to be 'They'll always let you down'. Only in the early twenty-first century did the club's badge and crest coincide.

STOKE – NO JOKE ...

If there's one team guaranteed to turn Albion fans as white as a sheet, it's Stoke City who have become something of a hoodoo side for the Baggies in recent years. After sending the Potters back home with a 6–0 Hawthorns drubbing in December 1988, City's jinx has been almost all-consuming in the past 21 years – here's the diabolical record since that happy occasion:

2008/09
Premier League
West Bromwich Albion 0–2 Stoke City

2008/09
Premier League
Stoke City 1–0 West Bromwich Albion

2007/08
Championship
Stoke City 3–1 West Bromwich Albion

2007/08
Championship
West Bromwich Albion 1–1 Stoke City

2006/07
Championship
West Bromwich Albion 1–3 Stoke City

2006/07
Championship
Stoke City 1–0 West Bromwich Albion

2003/04
League Division One
Stoke City 4–1 West Bromwich Albion

2003/04
League Division One
West Bromwich Albion 1–0 Stoke City

1997/98
FA Cup
West Bromwich Albion 3–1 Stoke City

1997/98
League Division One
West Bromwich Albion 1–1 Stoke City

1997/98
League Division One
Stoke City 0–0 West Bromwich Albion

1996/97
League Division One
Stoke City 2–1 West Bromwich Albion

1996/97
League Division One
West Bromwich Albion 0–2 Stoke City

1995/96
League Division One
West Bromwich Albion 0–1 Stoke City

1995/96
League Division One
Stoke City 2–1 West Bromwich Albion

1994/95
League Division One
West Bromwich Albion 1–3 Stoke City

1994/95
League Division One
Stoke City 4–1 West Bromwich Albion

1993/94
League Division One
West Bromwich Albion 0–0 Stoke City

1993/94
League Division One
Stoke City 1–0 West Bromwich Albion

1992/93
Associate Members' Cup
Stoke City 2–1 West Bromwich Albion

1992/93
League Division Two
West Bromwich Albion 1–2 Stoke City

1992/93
League Division Two
Stoke City 4–3 West Bromwich Albion

1991/92
Third Division
Stoke City 1–0 West Bromwich Albion

1991/92
Third Division
West Bromwich Albion 2–2 Stoke City

1989/90
Second Division
West Bromwich Albion 1–1 Stoke City

1989/90
Second Division
Stoke City 2–1 West Bromwich Albion

1988/89
Second Division
Stoke City 0–0 West Bromwich Albion

Those are the hard facts, here is the grisly breakdown – out of the past 27 meetings with our Oatcake-scoffing cousins, Stoke have won 18, drawn 7 and lost just twice. Albion have scored 22 and conceded 46. Albion have failed to win any of the last seven meetings, of which Stoke have emerged triumphant on all but one occasion. The only two meetings in the Premier League ended with Stoke winning both matches – their first Premiership away win was, of course, at The Hawthorns, ending an 11-match winless run . . . somebody make it stop!

KIT CABOODLE

The navy blue and white stripes that Albion have established as their team colours were not introduced until the 1885/86 season as the club had spent their formative years choosing which colours to settle on. In the 1880/81 season the club adopted a kit of red and blue quarters which then changed to yellow and white the following season. In the same year Albion mysteriously tried a kit of brown and blue halves which altered in the 1882/83 season to white and red hoops. In 1885, the club chose to implement a kit similar to the one of today and, though this was the first season that the 'Stripes' introduced their blue and white kit, the light blue differed to the present navy stripes. This kit was replaced following the First World War by an all-navy strip and though the club reverted back to stripes, the Second World War played a decisive role in further change of kit design. Due to rationing during the conflict, striped material became a luxury and as a result, the club was forced to reintroduce the all-navy kit.

For the majority of the Baggies' history, their second kit consisted of a white top and black shorts, yet this too was subject to change. The 1935 FA Cup final between Sheffield Wednesday and West Brom created a clash of colours and so Albion again played in the change navy strip. The defeat in the 1962 League Cup final ended a decade of an all-red second kit for the club and Baggies' fans will always remember the successful FA Cup run of 1968 and their all-white kit.

Albion's on-strip printing didn't begin until 1939 when the club included numbers on the backs of their jerseys and the club developed this design in 1969 when red numbers were incorporated onto the players' shorts. Ever since the 1981/82 season, West Brom have always had shirt sponsors, except for in exceptional circumstances like in 1994 when the club's law firm sponsors went bust. However, after T-Mobile's shirt sponsorship ended in the summer of 2008, Albion have played without any shirt sponsor and began the 2009/10 campaign as the only club in England to have just their badge and kit maker's emblem on the front of their shirt – much to the delight of most Baggies fans! One thing Albion fans can't stand is anyone suggested the boys play in black and white stripes . . . it's bloody NAVY and white! End of!

BAGGIES LEGEND – CYRILLE REGIS MBE

Although a future England international, Cyrille was born in French Guyana on 9 February 1958. Five years later he and his family moved to London, firstly to the Kensington area, prior to upping sticks and going to Stonebridge. His first foray into football came at school, where he was seen as an all-round sportsman, also participating in cricket and athletics. While at high school he was offered the opportunity to trial at Chelsea, but was unable to accept due to injury.

Regis did not walk straight into his famed profession, and was originally an electrician. Alongside his trade he was playing non-league football; his first club was Molesey where he had a successful period prior to leaving in acrimonious circumstances. Regis' second side was Hayes where he managed one season at the club, scoring 24 goals.

While turning out for the Isthmian League outfit he was spotted by West Brom chief scout Ronnie Allen who saw the potential of the young footballer, so much so that he offered to pay the original transfer fee himself as the club were not sure about signing the unproven striker. A £5,000 fee was paid for Regis and the man moved to the Midlands in the hope of making it in the professional game.

Soon after his arrival at WBA, a familiar face took over as manager of the first-team, when Ronnie Allen replaced Jonny Giles in the hot seat. Allen put him in the side for the League Cup game against Rotherham and Regis repaid the manager's faith in him by scoring twice in a 4–0 victory.

At The Hawthorns he was to become an integral part of the team, and was famously a member of the 'Three Degrees'. Regis, Laurie Cunningham and Brendan Batson never sang 'When Will I See You Again', but it might have been a good idea for the Baggies fans to start the chant at the end of each match, such was the pleasure they gave countless Albion supporters over the years. While at the club he was awarded the PFA Young Player of the Year award in 1978. By the end of his time at the Baggies he had amassed 112 goals in 301 appearances.

While at Albion he made his England debut by coming on as a substitute in a match against Northern Ireland in 1982. He went on to earn 4 more caps for his adopted nation, playing his last international match in 1987.

In 1984 Regis moved to Coventry City. He was an integral part of the team that won the FA Cup in 1987. He struggled to match his scoring record from his time at the Baggies, mainly due to the team's long-ball tactics, which did not suit Regis' power and speed – obviously a family trait with his cousin John Regis going on to win numerous medals for Great Britain for his 200m sprints. Even though City didn't play to his strengths, Regis managed to score 62 goals in 274 matches with the Sky Blues, before he was sold on to Aston Villa.

The forward arrived at Villa Park at the age of 33 and was coming towards the end of his career. He wasn't an automatic starter for the team and left the club after a year to play for Wolves – it was as if he was doing everything he could to turn the Baggies fans against him! His time at Molineux was equally unproductive as he failed to break-up the first choice strike partnership of Steve Bull and David Kelly, though every Albion fan believes that if he'd been presented with a chance to score against the Baggies, he'd have accidentally-on-purpose hit his shot wide.

He finished off his career with a period at Wycombe Wanderers before retiring at the age of 38 in 1996.

Since the end of his career as a professional footballer, Regis has worked as an agent, representing players like his nephew Jason Roberts. He has also received an honorary fellowship from the University of Wolverhampton in 2001. His other interests include charity work; along with his wife Julia he volunteers to work at WaterAid projects in Ethiopia. He also received the MBE in 2007.

HOME(S) SWEET HOME(S)

Albion's first home venue was a piece of enclosed ground known as Cooper's Hill, where the club played from 1878 to 1879; thereafter they seemed to play games at both Cooper's Hill and the adjacent Dartmouth Park up until 1881. Then it was off to Bunn's Field – known also as 'The Beeches' – on Walsall Street, where the playing staff and club officials carefully tended and rolled their new pitch, erected fences and added basic facilities in order to charge admission through a single turnstile to watch the Black Country's finest. They were attracting crowds averaging 400 before long (think Blues' away following!), but a year later, the Strollers were living up to their name as they again upped sticks and moved to their first enclosed ground at West Bromwich, Dartmouth Cricket Club's Four Acres, which had a capacity of around 2,000, from 1882 to 1885. The club charged three shillings for a season ticket and soon settled into their plush new surrounds, introducing a reserve team and thrashing a hapless Coseley 26–0 in the Birmingham Cup – still a club record, surprisingly(!).

From 1885 to 1900, the Baggies were resident at Stoney Lane after agreeing a 15-year lease at a cost of £25 per annum. The club enjoyed great times during their tenure at Stoney Lane, winning the FA Cup twice, but the Albion's popularity was causing problems – the ground was no longer large enough to hold the kind of crowds that wanted to watch the team and there was no way the venue could be expanded, located as it was among tightly-packed terraced streets.

The club began looking for a site for their very own stadium in 1886 and purchased a 10-acre site in an area known as 'The Hawthorns' – due in no small part to the masses of hawthorn bushes that were growing there. It was situated on the corner of Halfords Lane and the main Birmingham Road and on 3 September 1900, Albion played their first game at their newly-built ground, drawing 1–1 with Derby in front of a crowd of 20,104. The Hawthorns began life as it meant to go on, with Albion relegated at the end of their first season there!

Over the years, crowds as high as 64,000 watched games at the ground but the mid-1990s Taylor Report recommended all stadia become all-seater and the Baggies' capacity was reduced to 28,003. The current stands are known as the Birmingham Road End, Smethwick End, East Stand and West Stand. One trivia note worth including is that The Hawthorns' altitude of 551ft above sea level makes it the highest ground of all 92 League grounds in England, so don't forget your oxygen at the next home game and remember to save your pie crusts for the mountain goats that can be seen grazing around the car parks. . . .

I PREDICT A RIOT . . .

Go on, admit it – you thought hooligans first raised their neanderthal heads back in the early 1970s, didn't you? Wrong. The first recorded crowd disturbances were during the November 1882 Staffordshire Cup tie against the Villa at Perry Barr. Playing against such well-established neighbours as Villa (formed five years earlier!), West Brom fans and players endured a shower of stones and clods of earth at their arrival at Villa from the locals – nothing much has changed, then! Our arrogant neighbours couldn't help but sneer at the runts of Midlands football and put out a scratch team, though it was the 3,000 travelling Albion fans who left smiling after a heroic 3–3 draw.

WIDE A WAKE CLUB

Towards the end of the 1800s it was a Black Country custom to make the first Monday of November 'Wake Monday'. Pubs would lay on cheap beer and food and most workers were given the day off. Forward-thinking Albion began to re-arrange home League fixtures to fall on this unofficial Bank Holiday (of sorts) and from 1887 to 1897 Albion exclusively played Bolton Wanderers on

Wake Monday, all played at Stoney Lane. The Baggies won just 4 of those 11 games, losing 6 and drawing the other until the last 3 games in 1888, 1889 and 1900 were played against Everton, Sheffield United and Stoke City – the latter being the only time the Wake Monday game was played at The Hawthorns. From 1901 onwards the club returned to its normal November schedule.

CHEAPER BY THE DOZEN?

One of the most famous results in English football occurred on 4 April 1892 when the Baggies destroyed Lancastrian outfit Darwen 12–0 at Stoney Lane. Albion were on fire that day and it is only fitting that the goalscorers who etched the club's name into the history books for the biggest top-flight victory ever, are repeated here:

1–0:   Tom Pearson
2–0:   John Reynolds
3–0:   Billy Bassett
4–0:   John Reynolds
5–0:   Tom Pearson
Half time: Albion 5 Darwen 0
6–0:   Billy Bassett
7–0:   Billy Bassett
8–0:   Tom Pearson
9–0:   Hunt (own goal – as if it wasn't bad enough!)
10–0:   Tom Pearson
11–0:   Jasper Geddes
12–0:   Sammy Nicholls

Albion line up: Reader, J. Horton, McCulloch, Reynolds, C. Perry, Groves, Bassett, McLeod, Nicholls, Pearson, Geddes
Attendance: 1,109

Ironically, Albion went into the game without a win in 5 games during which they'd picked up 1 point. Twelve days later the teams met again, with Darwen clawing back some pride with a 1–1 draw on their own patch. The Baggies fans certainly know how to pick a game, too – this was the lowest home gate of the season!

SKINNERISMS

Frank Skinner, Albion's most famous fan – though no doubt he cringes at the title – is never short of a few words on his beloved Baggies. Here are a few pearlers:

'I'd love to have my ashes scattered at The Hawthorns. Just imagine in the winter having the under-soil heating filtering through you. I'm not sure if they still do it though. If not, I'll have to do it sneakily. As I get older I could start having bits removed, incinerated and steadily start the process myself. . . .'

Frank on his ideal future resting place

'As you get older you get your priorities straight. I don't have children but I have the Albion.'

Frank admits to having sleepless nights all the same

'It was at home to Southampton – the rain was torrential and there were no goals. But I was hooked.'

Recalling his first game

'I'll watch it, obviously, but I'd much rather Albion stay up than England win the World Cup. No contest at all.'

Frank Skinner – a Baggie till he dies

'Recently, when one of our players blasted the ball over the bar, I heard one say, "I wouldn't have liked to have him on the three-inch-mortars." It made me laugh because it's basically a heckle from the Second World War! You don't hear enough of those these days.'

On timeless humour

'I wouldn't usually wear this, I'm usually more of a scarf man myself. I think the clubs only encourage us to wear replica shirts because they know our mums can't knit them.'

Frank on wearing a club shirt on matchdays

'I used to have a daydream about playing for Albion that I'd only indulge in when I was on the toilet. It was a very involved fantasy and went on for a whole string of craps, if that's the correct collective noun for craps.'

Too much information?

'Someone called from the crowd "Is it true you're selling your shed, Willie?" They did a negotiation and he sealed the deal. I fell in love with him.'

Frank reveals the identity of his favourite Albion player – Willie Johnston

'We are the yin and yang of West Bromwich Albion. We've got seats on the halfway line, I'm just one side and he's the other, it's like the Greenwich Meridian. When they come out to warm up he says, "Oh, they don't look right today." At 3–0 down, I've heard myself say, "A lot can happen in four minutes."'

Skinnner and Adrian Chiles – the Waldorf and Stadler of The Hawthorns

SEAL OF APPROVAL?

Apparently, the reason Villa fans have been called 'seals' over the years can be traced back to Mike Thomas, former treasurer of WBASC, who witnessed Villa supporters in the old wooden Trinity Road stand clapping and stamping the wooden floor at the same time while shrieking in a falsetto voice 'Villa!' This apparently reminded him of a seal, he mentioned it to a few mates, the name took off and a whole mythology built up around claret and blue, fish and beach balls.

PENALTY!

Albion's first penalty kick in a competitive game was awarded in April 1892 in the Division One clash with Nottingham Forest. John Reynolds successfully converted the kick to level the score and earn the Baggies a 2–2 draw.

Of course, the Baggies wouldn't be the Baggies if they hadn't missed their first EVER penalty kick. That came three months earlier on 11 January when Tom Pearson blasted the ball over the bar during a friendly against Villa. Worse still, the first penalty conceded by Albion was against Wolves, just days after the penalty kick rule had been introduced by the FA. Happily, it was fluffed and narrowly missed a passing gull.

In 1911/12, keeper Hubert Pearson scored twice from the spot during victories over Middlesbrough and Bury while fellow custodian Jim Sanders was more active at the other end, saving an incredible 20 penalties for Albion. The greatest spot-taker of them all was Tony Brown, who slotted home 53 penalties during his Baggies career, though this includes friendlies. Ronnie Allen's 40 successes are worth mentioning, too.

ALL'S FAIR IN EUROPEAN COMPETITION

Victory in the 1966 League Cup final meant Albion qualified for European competition for the first time in the club's history and in the 1966/67 season the Baggies entered the Fairs Cup – later to be renamed the UEFA Cup – and were awarded a bye in the first round. Albion were then pitted against Dutch side Utrecht in the second round and after earning a 1–1 draw in Holland with Bob Hope (no kidding!) scoring a vital away goal, Albion turned on the style at The Hawthorns winning the return 5–2 during which Tony Brown scored a hat-trick and a penalty – two firsts for the club. Bologna, who seemed to have played all 92 English clubs at some point during the ill-fated Anglo-Italian Cup, were next up, but proved to be too savvy for the relatively inexperienced Baggies and romped home 6–1 on aggregate after winning 3–0 in Italy and then triumphing 3–1 at The Hawthorns.

Fairs Cup record:

1966/67
R1 Bye
R2 (leg 1)   Utrecht (A)   1–1
R2 (leg 2)   Utrecht (H)   5–2
R3 (leg 1)   Bologna (A)   0–3
R3 (leg 2)   Bologna (H)   1–3

Pld: 4   W: 1   D: 1   L: 2   F: 7   A: 9

EUROPEAN CUP WINNERS' CUP

A season passed before Albion were again involved in Europe, this time in the European Cup Winners' Cup after winning the FA Cup the previous May.

In the first round, Albion looked to be heading out after a 3–1 defeat to Club Brugge of Belgium. More than 33,000 fans cheered on the Albion in the return and goals from Asa Hartford (who'd scored the vital away goal) and Tony Brown were enough to send the Baggies through on the away goals rule.

Next up were Romanian side Dinamo Bucharest and again Hartford grabbed a vital away goal during a creditable 1–1 draw. Albion, again watched by more than 33,000 fans, romped home 4–0 in the return to move into the quarter-finals where the might of European giants Dunfermline awaited. The Scottish outfit were lying fourth in Division One – they weren't even an SPL side and surely would be swept aside.

Albion played the first leg in Scotland with caution, returning south with a 0–0 draw, but the expected progression into the semis never materialised as the Scots left with a 1–0 victory, leaving the near (again) 33,000 crowd to wonder about what might have been. Dunfermline, for the record, were dispatched 2–1 on aggregate by Slovan Bratislava in the semis.

European Cup Winners' Cup record:

1968/69
R1 (leg 1) Club Brugge (A)   1–3
R1 (leg 2) Club Brugge (H)   2–0
R2 (leg 1) Dinamo Bucharest (A)   1–1
R2 (leg 2) Dinamo Bucharest (H)   4–0

QF (leg 1) Dunfermline Ath (A)   0–0
QF (leg 2) Dunfermline Ath (H)   0–1
Pld: 6   W: 2   D: 2   L: 2   F: 8   A: 5

UEFA CUP

Big Ron's Albion went into the 1978/79 UEFA Cup on the crest of a wave after finishing sixth the previous season in the top flight. They were drawn in the first round to face the cauldron that is Galatasaray away, but inspired by Laurie Cunningham who grabbed two goals, Albion recorded a magnificent 3–1 win in Turkey to render the return leg all but a formality.

For once, the Baggies strayed from the script and won The Hawthorns leg 3–1 before dispatching Portuguese opposition in the second round by beating Sporting Braga 2–0 away and 1–0 at home.

The third round pitted Atkinson's men with arguably their toughest ever European opponent (Dunfermline apart) when they took on La Liga giants Valencia. It was Cunningham who again led the opposition a merry dance and his vital away goal at the Madrigals Stadium earned a 1–1 draw for the Baggies and gave them a terrific chance of moving into the last eight. The Spaniards found Albion in the middle of a red-hot run that would yield 10 League wins and 2 draws and the 2–0 win, again with Cunningham in imperious form, confirmed Big Ron's theory that, at that particular time, Albion were probably as good as any team in Europe.

For the quarter-final, the Baggies were still gunning for the League title with Liverpool and in red-hot form, but the draw against Red Star Belgrade was particularly tough. The first leg in Yugoslavia attracted 95,300 partisan fans and amid the charged atmosphere, the hosts edged the match 1–0. Cyrille Regis sent The Hawthorns wild by levelling the aggregate scores in the return leg, but a late Belgrade goal saw the visitors through 2–1 overall and dumped perhaps the greatest Albion side ever out of the competition. Such dizzy heights were never repeated in the next two ventures into Europe with German side Carl Zeiss Jena and Grasshoppers Zurich winning both legs in successive round knock outs in 1979 and 1980. The complete UEFA Cup record is:

1978/79

R1 (leg 1) Galatasaray (A)	3–1
R1 (leg 2) Galatasaray (H)	3–1
R2 (leg 1) Sporting Braga (A)	2–0
R2 (leg 2) Sporting Braga (H)	1–0
R3 (leg 1) Valencia (A)	1–1
R3 (leg 2) Valencia (H)	2–0
QF (leg 1) Red Star Belgrade (A)	0–1
QF (leg 2) Red Star Belgrade (H)	1–1

1979/80

R1 (leg 1) Carl Zeiss Jena (A)	0–2
R1 (leg 2) Carl Zeiss Jena (H)	1–2

1981/82

R1 (leg 1) Grasshoppers Zurich (A)	0–1
R1 (leg 2) Grasshoppers Zurich (H)	1–3

Pld: 12   W: 5   D: 2   L: 5   F: 15   A: 13

Total European record:
Pld: 22   W: 8   D: 5   L: 9   F: 30   A: 27

BIG RONISMS – VOLUME 2

More priceless quotes from the Cuprinol King – explanations rendered pointless:

'They've done the old-fashioned things well; they've kicked the ball, they've headed it . . .'

'They've picked their heads up off the ground, and they now have a lot to carry on their shoulders.'

'Well, either side could win it, or it could be a draw.'

'He sliced the ball when he had it on a plate.'

'I'm afraid they've left their legs at home.'

'The keeper was unsighted – he still didn't see it.'

'Zero-zero is a big score.'

'You half-fancied that to go in as it was rising and dipping at the same time.'

'Chelsea look like they've got a couple more gears left in the locker.'

'Now Manchester United are 2–1 down on aggregate, they are in a better position than when they started the game at 1–1.'

'Huddersfield will want to win this one.'

'That was Pelé's strength – holding people off with his arm.'

'Stoitchkov's playing on the wing, in this situation he likes to come in and scalp the centre-half.'

'He's the equivalent of the Spanish David Beckham.'

'A ten-foot keeper really should have stopped that.'

'There's a little triangle – five left-footed players.'

'I tell you what; if the Cameroons get a goal back here they're literally gonna catch on fire.'

'Well, Clive, it's all about the two Ms – movement and positioning.'

'He must be lightning slow.'

'There's a snap about Liverpool that just isn't there.'

'For me their biggest threat is when they get into the attacking part of the field.'

'If you score against the Italians you deserve a goal.'

THE FA CUP – THE BAGGIES' COMPLETE RECORD

1884/85
R4   Druids   H 1–0
R5   Bye
QF   Blackburn Rovers   H 0–2

1885/86
R3   Bye
R4   Wolverhampton Wanderers   H 3–1
R5   Old Carthusians H 1–0
QF   Old Westminsters   H 6–0
SF   Small Heath Alliance   N 4–0
                    (played at Aston Lower Grounds)
F   Blackburn Rovers   N 0–0
                    (played at Kennington Oval)
Fr   Blackburn Rovers   N 0–2
                    (played at Racecourse Ground, Derby)

1886/87
R3   Bye
R4   Mitchell St George's   A 1–0
R5   Lockwood Brothers   A 1–0
                    (replay ordered after protest)
R5r Lockwood Brothers   N 2–1
                    (played at Derby Cricket Ground)
QF   Notts County   A 4–1
SF   Preston North End   N 3–1
                    (played at Trent Bridge, Nottingham)
F   Aston Villa   N 0–2
                    (played at Kennington Oval)

1887/88

R3	Wolverhampton Wanderers	H 2–0
R4	Bye	
R5	Stoke City	H 4–1
QF	Old Carthusians	H 4–2
SF	Derby Junction	N 3–0
		(played at Stoke)
F	Preston North End	N 2–1
		(played at Kennington Oval)

1888/89

R1	Small Heath Alliance	A 3–2
R2	Burnley	H 5–1
QF	Chatham	H 10–1
SF	Preston North End	N 0–1
		(played at Sheffield United)

1889/90

R1	Accrington FC	A 1–3
		(declared void)
R1	Accrington FC	A 0–3

1890/91

R1	Old Westminsters	H (walkover)
R2	Birmingham St George's	A 3–0
QF	Sheffield Wednesday	A 2–0
SF	Blackburn Rovers	N 2–3
		(played at Stoke)

1891/92

R1	Old Westminsters	A 3–2
R2	Blackburn Rovers	H 3–1
QF	Sheffield Wednesday	H 2–1
SF	Nottingham Forest	N 1–1
		(played at Wolverhampton Wanderers)

SFr	Nottingham Forest	N 1–1
	(played at Wolverhampton Wanderers)	
SFr2	Nottingham Forest	N 6–2
	(played at Derby County)	
F	Aston Villa	N 3–0
	(played at Kennington Oval)	

1892/93

| R1 | Everton | A 1–4 |

1893/94

| R1 | Blackburn Rovers | H 2–3 |

1894/95

R1	Small Heath Alliance	A 2–1
R2	Sheffield United	A 1–1
R2r	Sheffield United	H 2–1
QF	Wolverhampton Wanderers	H 1–0
SF	Sheffield Wednesday	N 0–2
	(played at Derby Cricket Ground)	
F	Aston Villa	N 0–1
	(played at Crystal Palace)	

1895/96

R1	Blackburn Rovers	A 2–1
R2	Grimsby Town	A 1–1
R2r	Grimsby Town	H 3–0
QF	Derby County	A 0–1

1896/97

| R1 | Luton Town | A 1–0 |
| R2 | Liverpool | H 1–2 |

1897/98

R1	New Brighton Tower	H 2–0
R2	Sheffield Wednesday	H 1–0
QF	Nottingham Forest	H 2–3

1898/99

R1	South Shore	H 8–0
R2	Bury	H 2–1
QF	Liverpool	H 0–2

1899/00

R1	Walsall	A 1–1
R1r	Walsall	H 6–1
R2	Liverpool	A 1–1
R2r	Liverpool	H 2–1
QF	Southampton	A 1–2

1900/01

R1	Manchester City	H 1–0
R2	Woolwich Arsenal	A 1–0
QF	Middlesbrough	A 1–0
SF	Tottenham Hotspur	N 0–4
		(played at Aston Villa)

1901/02

| R1 | Bury | A 1–5 |

1902/03

| R1 | Tottenham Hotspur | A 0–0 |
| R1r | Tottenham Hotspur | H 0–2 |

1903/04

| R1 | Nottingham Forest | H 1–1 |
| R1r | Nottingham Forest | A 1–3 |

1904/05
Intermediate round
Leicester Fosse   H 2–5

1905/06
R1   Everton   A 1–3

1906/07
R1   Stoke City   H 1–1
R1r   Stoke City   A 2–2
R1r2   Stoke City   N 2–0
                                   (played at Aston Villa)
R2   Norwich City   H 1–0
R3   Derby County   H 2–0
QF   Notts County   H 3–1
SF   Everton   N 1–2
                                   (played at Bolton Wanderers)

1907/08
R1   Birmingham City   H 1–1
R1r   Birmingham City   A 2–1
R2   Southampton   A 0–1

1908/09
R1   Bolton Wanderers   H 3–1
R2   Bradford City   H 1–2

1909/10
R1   Clapton Orient   H 2–0
R2   Bristol City   A 1–1
R2r   Bristol City   H 4–2
R3   Barnsley   A 0–1

1910/11

| R1 | Fulham | H 4–1 |
| R2 | Derby County | A 0–2 |

1911/12

R1	Tottenham Hotspur	H 3–0
R2	Leeds City	A 1–0
R3	Sunderland	A 2–1
QF	Fulham	H 3–0
SF	Blackburn Rovers	N 0–0
		(played at Liverpool)
SFr	Blackburn Rovers	N 1–0
		(played at Sheffield Wednesday)
F	Barnsley	N 0–0
		(played at Crystal Palace)
F	Barnsley	N 0–1
		(played at Sheffield United)

1912/13

R1	West Ham United	H 1–1
R1r	West Ham United	A 2–2
R1r2	West Ham United	N 0–3
		(played at Chelsea)

1913/14

R1	Grimsby Town	H 2–0
R2	Leeds City	A 2–0
R3	Aston Villa	A 1–2

1914/15

| R1 | Hull City | A 0–1 |

1919/20

| R1 | Barnsley | H 0–1 |

1920/21
R1	Notts County	A 0–3

1921/22
R1	Chelsea	A 4–2
R2	Liverpool	A 1–0
R3	Notts County	H 1–1
R3r	Notts County	A 0–2

1922/23
R1	Stalybridge Celtic	H 0–0
R1r	Stalybridge Celtic	A 2–0
R2	Sunderland	H 2–1
R3	Charlton Athletic	A 0–1

1923/24
R1	Millwall	A 1–0
R2	Corinthians	H 5–0
R3	Wolverhampton Wanderers	H 1–1
R3r	Wolverhampton Wanderers	A 2–0
QF	Aston Villa	H 0–2

1924/25
R1	Luton Town	H 4–0
R2	Preston North End	H 2–0
R3	Aston Villa	H 1–1
R3r	Aston Villa	A 2–1
QF	Sheffield United	A 0–2

1925/26
R3	Bristol City	H 4–1
R4	Aston Villa	H 1–2

1926/27

R3   Hull City   A 1–2

1927/28

R3   Arsenal   A 0–2

1928/29

R3   Grimsby Town   A 1–1
R3r   Grimsby Town   H 2–0
R4   Middlesbrough   H 1–0
R5   Bradford Park Avenue   H 6–0
QF   Huddersfield Town   H 1–1
QFr   Huddersfield Town   A 1–2

1929/30

R3   Wrexham   A 0–1

1930/31

R3   Charlton Athletic   H 2–2
R3r   Charlton Athletic   A 1–1
R3r2 Charlton Athletic   N 3–1
                                       (played at Aston Villa)
R4   Tottenham Hotspur   H 1–0
R5   Portsmouth   A 1–0
QF   Wolverhampton Wanderers   H 1–1
QFr   Wolverhampton Wanderers   A 2–1
SF   Everton   N 1–0
                                       (played at Manchester United)
F   Birmingham City   N 2–1
                                       (played at Wembley)

1931/32

R3   Aston Villa   H 1–2

1932/33

R3	Liverpool	H 2–0
R4	West Ham United	A 0–2

1933/34

R3	Chelsea	A 1–1
R3r	Chelsea	H 0–1

1934/35

R3	Port Vale	H 2–1
R4	Sheffield United	H 7–1
R5	Stockport County	A 5–0
QF	Preston North End	H 1–0
SF	Bolton Wanderers	N 1–1
		(played at Leeds United)
SFr	Bolton Wanderers	N 2–0
		(played at Stoke City)
F	Sheffield Wednesday	N 2–4
		(played at Wembley)

1935/36

R3	Hull City	H 2–0
R4	Bradford Park Avenue	A 1–1
R4r	Bradford Park Avenue	H 1–1
R4r2	Bradford Park Avenue	N 0–2
		(played at Manchester United)

1936/37

R3	Spennymoor United	H 7–1
R4	Darlington	H 3–2
R5	Coventry City	A 3–2
QF	Arsenal	H 3–1
SF	Preston North End	N 1–4
		(played at Arsenal)

1937/38

R3	Newcastle United	H 1–0
R4	York City	A 2–3

1938/39

R3	Manchester United	H 0–0
R3r	Manchester United	A 5–1
R4	Portsmouth	A 0–2

1945/46

R3(1)	Cardiff City	A 1–1
R3(2)	Cardiff City	H 4–0
R4(1)	Derby County	A 0–1
R4(2)	Derby County	H 1–3

1946/47

R3	Leeds United	H 2–1
R4	Charlton Athletic	H 1–2

1947/48

R3	Reading	H 2–0
R4	Tottenham Hotspur	A 1–3

1948/49

R3	Lincoln City	A 1–0
R4	Gateshead	A 3–1
R5	Chelsea	H 3–0
QF	Wolverhampton Wanderers	A 0–1

1949/50

R3	Cardiff City	A 2–2
R3r	Cardiff City	H 0–1

1950/51

| R3 | Derby County | A 2–2 |
| R3r | Derby County | H 0–1 |

1951/52

R3	Bolton Wanderers	H 4–0
R4	Gateshead	A 2–0
		(played at Newcastle United)
R5	Blackburn Rovers	A 0–1

1952/53

R3	West Ham United	A 4–1
R4	Chelsea	A 1–1
R4r	Chelsea	H 0–0
R4r2	Chelsea	N 1–1
		(played at Aston Villa)
R4r3	Chelsea	N 0–4
		(played at Arsenal)

1953/54

R3	Chelsea	H 1–0
R4	Rotherham United	H 4–0
R5	Newcastle United	H 3–2
QF	Tottenham Hotspur	H 3–0
SF	Port Vale	N 2–1
		(played at Aston Villa)
F	Preston North End	N 3–2
		(played at Wembley)

1954/55

| R3 | Bournemouth & Boscombe | A 1–0 |
| R4 | Charlton Athletic | H 2–4 |

1955/56

R3	Wolverhampton Wanderers	A 2–1
R4	Portsmouth	H 2–0
R5	Birmingham City	H 0–1

1956/57

R3	Doncaster Rovers	A 1–1
R3r	Doncaster Rovers	H 2–0
R4	Sunderland	H 4–2
R5	Blackpool	A 0–0
R5r	Blackpool	H 2–1
QF	Arsenal	H 2–2
QFr	Arsenal	A 2–1
SF	Aston Villa	N 2–2
SFr	Aston Villa	N 0–1

1957/58

R3	Manchester City	H 5–1
R4	Nottingham Forest	H 3–3
R4r	Nottingham Forest	A 5–1
R5	Sheffield United	A 1–1
R5r	Sheffield United	H 4–1
QF	Manchester United	H 2–2
QFr	Manchester United	A 0–1

1958/59

R3	Sheffield Wednesday	A 2–0
R4	Brentford	H 2–0
R5	Blackpool	A 1–3

1959/60

R3	Plymouth Argyle	H 3–2
R4	Bolton Wanderers	H 2–0
R5	Leicester City	A 1–2

1960/61

R3	Lincoln City	A 1–3

1961/62

R3	Blackpool	A 0–0
R3r	Blackpool	H 4–1
R4	Wolverhampton Wanderers	A 2–1
R5	Tottenham Hotspur	H 2–4

1962/63

R3	Plymouth Argyle	A 5–1
R4	Nottingham Forest	H 0–0
R4r	Nottingham Forest	A 1–2

1963/64

R3	Blackpool	H 2–2
R3r	Blackpool	A 1–0
R4	Arsenal	H 3–3
R4r	Arsenal	A 0–2

1964/65

R3	Liverpool	H 1–2

1965/66

R3	Bolton Wanderers	A 0–3

1966/67

R3	Northampton Town	A 3–1
R4	Leeds United	A 0–5

1967/68

R3	Colchester United	A 1–1
R3r	Colchester United	H 4–0
R4	Southampton	H 1–1
R4r	Southampton	A 3–2

R5	Portsmouth	A 2–1
QF	Liverpool	H 0–0
QFr	Liverpool	A 1–1
QFr2	Liverpool	N 2–1
		(played at Manchester City)
SF	Birmingham City	N 2–0
		(played at Aston Villa)
F	Everton	N 1–0
		(played at Wembley)

1968/69

R3	Norwich City	H 3–0
R4	Fulham	A 2–1
R5	Arsenal	H 1–0
QF	Chelsea	A 2–1
SF	Leicester City	N 0–1
		(played at Sheffield Wednesday)

1969/70

| R3 | Sheffield Wednesday | A 1–2 |

1970/71

R3	Scunthorpe United	H 0–0
R3r	Scunthorpe United	A 3–1
R4	Ipswich Town	H 1–1
R4r	Ipswich Town	A 0–3

1971/72

| R3 | Coventry City | H 1–2 |

1972/73

R3	Nottingham Forest	H 1–1
R3r	Nottingham Forest	A 0–0
R3r2	Nottingham Forest	N 3–1
		(played at Leicester City)

| R4 | Swindon Town | H 2–0 |
| R5 | Leeds United | A 0–2 |

1973/74

R3	Notts County	H 4–0
R4	Everton	A 0–0
R4r	Everton	H 1–0
R5	Newcastle United	H 0–3

1974/75

R3	Bolton Wanderers	A 0–0
R3r	Bolton Wanderers	H 4–0
R4	Carlisle United	A 2–3

1975/76

R3	Carlisle United	H 3–1
R4	Lincoln City	H 3–2
R5	Southampton	H 1–1
R5r	Southampton	A 0–4

1976/77

| R3 | Manchester City | A 1–1 |
| R3r | Manchester City | H 0–1 |

1977/78

R3	Blackpool	H 4–1
R4	Manchester United	A 1–1
R4r	Manchester United	H 3–2
R5	Derby County	A 3–2
QF	Nottingham Forest	H 2–0
SF	Ipswich Town	N 1–3
		(played at Arsenal)

1978/79

R3	Coventry City	A 2–2
R3r	Coventry City	H 4–0
R4	Leeds United	A 3–3
		(played at West Bromwich Albion)
R4r	Leeds United	H 2–0
R5	Southampton	H 1–1
R5r	Southampton	A 1–2

1979/80

R3	West Ham United	H 1–1
R3r	West Ham United	A 1–2

1980/81

R3	Grimsby Town	H 3–0
R4	Middlesbrough	A 0–1

1981/82

R3	Blackburn Rovers	H 3–2
R4	Gillingham	A 1–0
R5	Norwich City	H 1–0
QF	Coventry City	H 2–0
SF	QPR	N 0–1
		(played at Arsenal)

1982/83

R3	QPR	H 3–2
R4	Tottenham Hotspur	A 1–2

1983/84

R3	Rotherham United	A 0–0
R3r	Rotherham United	H 3–0
R4	Scunthorpe United	H 1–0
R5	Plymouth Argyle	H 0–1

1984/85

| R3 | Leyton Orient | A 1–2 |

1985/86

| R3 | Sheffield Wednesday | A 2–2 |
| R3r | Sheffield Wednesday | H 2–3 |

1986/87

| R3 | Swansea City | A 2–3 |

1987/88

| R3 | Wimbledon | A 1–4 |

1988/89

| R3 | Everton | H 1–1 |
| R3r | Everton | A 0–1 |

1989/90

R3	Wimbledon	H 2–0
R4	Charlton Athletic	H 1–0
R5	Aston Villa	H 0–2

1990/91

| R3 | Woking | H 2–4 |

1991/92

| R1 | Marlow | H 6–0 |
| R2 | Leyton Orient | A 1–2 |

1992/93

R1	Aylesbury United	H 8–0
R2	Wycombe Wanderers	A 2–2
R2r	Wycombe Wanderers	H 1–0
R3	West Ham United	H 0–2

1993/94
| R1 | Halifax Town | A 1–2 |

1994/95
| R3 | Coventry City | A 1–1 |
| R3r | Coventry City | H 1–2 |

1995/96
| R3 | Crewe Alexandra | A 3–4 |

1996/97
| R3 | Chelsea | A 0–3 |

1997/98
| R3 | Stoke City | H 3–1 |
| R4 | Aston Villa | A 0–4 |

1998/99
| R3 | Bournemouth | A 0–1 |

1999/2000
| R3 | Blackburn Rovers | H 2–2 |
| R3r | Blackburn Rovers | A 0–2 |

2000/01
| R3 | Derby County | A 2–3 |

2001/02
R3	Sunderland	A 2–1
R4	Leicester City	H 1–0
R5	Cheltenham Town	H 1–0
QF	Fulham	H 0–1

2002/03

R3	Bradford City	H 3–1
R4	Watford	A 0–1

2003/04

R3	Nottingham Forest	A 0–1

2004/05

R3	Preston North End	A 2–0
R4	Tottenham Hotspur	H 1–1
R4r	Tottenham Hotspur	A 1–3

2005/06

R3	Reading	H 1–1
R3r	Reading	A 2–3

2006/07

R3	Leeds United	H 3–1
R4	Wolverhampton Wanderers	A 3–0
R5	Middlesbrough	A 2–2
R5r	Middlesbrough	H 1–1

(Middlesbrough won on pens)

2007/08

R3	Charlton Athletic	A 1–1
R3r	Charlton Athletic	H 2–2

(Albion won on pens)

R4	Peterborough United	A 3–0
R5	Coventry City	A 5–0
R6	Bristol Rovers	A 5–1
SF	Portsmouth	N 0–1

(played at Wembley)

2008/09

R3	Peterborough United	H 1–1
R3r	Peterborough United	A 2–0
R4	Burnley	H 2–2
R4r	Burnley	A 1–3

FOOTBALL LEAGUE CUP

1965/66

R2	Walsall	H 3–1
R3	Leeds United	A 4–2
R4	Coventry City	A 1–1
R4r	Coventry City	H 6–1
QF	Aston Villa	H 3–1
SF(1)	Peterborough United	H 2–1
SF(2)	Peterborough United	A 4–2
	(West Brom won 6–3 on agg)	
F(1)	West Ham United	A 1–2
F(2)	West Ham United	H 4–1
	(West Brom won 5–3 on agg)	

1966/67

R2	Aston Villa	H 6–1
R3	Manchester City	H 4–2
R4	Swindon Town	A 2–0
QF	Northampton Town	A 3–1
SF(1)	West Ham United	H 4–0
SF(2)	West Ham United	A 2–2
	(West Brom won 6–2 on agg)	
F	QPR	N 2–3
	(played at Wembley)	

1967/68

R2	Reading	A 1–3

1968/69

R2	Nottingham Forest	A 3–2
		(played at Notts County)
R3	Peterborough United	A 1–2

1969/70

R2	Aston Villa	A 2–1
R3	Ipswich Town	A 1–1
R3r	Ipswich Town	H 2–0
R4	Bradford City	H 4–0
QF	Leicester City	A 0–0
QFr	Leicester City	H 2–1
SF(1)	Carlisle United	A 0–1
SF(2)	Carlisle United	H 4–1
		(West Brom won 4–2 on agg)
F	Manchester City	N 1–2
		(played at Wembley)

1970/71

R2	Charlton Athletic	H 3–1
R3	Preston North End	A 1–0
R4	Tottenham Hotspur	A 0–5

1971/72

R2	Tottenham Hotspur	H 0–1

1

1972/73

R2	QPR	H 2–1
R3	Liverpool	H 1–1
R3r	Liverpool	A 1–2

1973/74

R2	Sheffield United	H 2–1
R3	Exeter City	H 1–3

1974/75

R2	Millwall	H 1–0
R3	Norwich City	H 1–1
R3r	Norwich City	A 0–2

1975/76

R2	Fulham	H 1–1
R2r	Fulham	A 0–1

1976/77

R2	Liverpool	A 1–1
R2r	Liverpool	H 1–0
R3	Brighton & Hove Albion	H 0–2

1977/78

R2	Rotherham United	H 4–0
R3	Watford	H 1–0
R4	Bury	A 0–1

1978/79

R2	Leeds United	H 0–0
R2r	Leeds United	A 0–0
R2r2	Leeds United	N 0–1
		(played at Manchester City)

1979/80

R2(1) Fulham		H 1–1
R2(2) Fulham		A 1–0
		(West Brom won 2–1 on agg)
R3	Coventry City	H 2–1
R4	Norwich City	H 0–0
R4r	Norwich City	A 0–3

1980/81

R2(1)	Leicester City	H 1–0
R2(2)	Leicester City	A 1–0
		(West Brom won 2–0 on agg)
R3	Everton	A 2–1
R4	Preston North End	H 0–0
R4r	Preston North End	A 1–1
R4r2	Preston North End	H 2–1
QF	Manchester City	A 1–2

1981/82

R2(1)	Shrewsbury Town	A 3–3
R2(2)	Shrewsbury Town	H 2–1
		(West Brom won 5–4 on agg)
R3	West Ham United	A 2–2
R3r	West Ham United	H 1–1
R3r2	West Ham United	A 1–0
R4	Crystal Palace	A 3–1
QF	Aston Villa	A 1–0
SF(1)	Tottenham Hotspur	H 0–0
SF(2)	Tottenham Hotspur	A 0–1
		(Tottenham won 1–0 on agg)

1982/83

R2(1)	Nottingham Forest	A 1–6
R2(2)	Nottingham Forest	H 3–1
		(Forest won 7–4 on agg)

1983/84

R2(1)	Millwall	A 0–3
R2(2)	Millwall	H 5–1
		(West Brom won 5–4 on agg)
R3	Chelsea	A 1–0
R4	Aston Villa	H 1–2

1984/85

R2(1) Wigan Athletic	A 0–0
R2(2) Wigan Athletic	H 3–1
	(West Brom won 3–1 on agg)
R3 Birmingham City	A 0–0
R3r Birmingham City	H 3–1
R4 Watford	A 1–4

1985/86

R2(1) Port Vale	H 1–0
R2(2) Port Vale	A 2–2
	(West Brom won 3–2 on agg)
R3 Coventry City	A 0–0
R3r Coventry City	H 4–3
R4 Aston Villa	A 2–2
R4r Aston Villa	H 1–2

1986/87

R2(1) Derby County	A 1–4
R2(2) Derby County	H 0–1
	(Derby County won 5–1 on agg)

1987/88

R1(1) Walsall	H 2–3
R1(2) Walsall	A 0–0
	(Walsall won 3–2 on agg)

1988/89

R1(1) Peterborough United	H 0–3
R1(2) Peterborough United	A 2–0
	(Peterborough won 3–2 on agg)

1989/90

R2(1) Bradford City		H 1–3
R2(2) Bradford City		A 5–3
	(Agg 6–6 – Albion won on away goals)	
R3	Newcastle United	A 1–0
R4	Derby County	A 0–2

1990/91

R1(1) Bristol City	H 2–2
R1(2) Bristol City	A 0–1
	(Bristol City won 3–2 on agg)

1991/92

R1(1) Swindon Town	A 0–2
R1(2) Swindon Town	H 2–2
	(Swindon Town won 4–2 on agg)

1992/93

R1(1) Plymouth Argyle	H 1–0
R1(2) Plymouth Argyle	A 0–2
	(Plymouth Argyle won 2–1 on agg)

1993/94

R1(1) Bristol Rovers	A 4–1
R1(2) Bristol Rovers	H 0–0
	(West Brom won 4–1 on agg)
R2(1) Chelsea	H 1–1
R2(2) Chelsea	A 1–2
	(Chelsea won 3–2 on agg)

1994/95

R1(1) Hereford United	A 0–0
R1(2) Hereford United	H 0–1
	(Hereford United won 1–0 on agg)

1995/96

R1(1) Northampton Town	H 1–1
R1(2) Northampton Town	A 4–2
	(West Brom won 5–3 on agg)
R2(1) Reading	A 1–1
R2(2) Reading	H 2–4
	(Reading won 5–3 on agg)

1996/97

R1(1) Colchester United	A 3–2
R1(2) Colchester United	H 1–3
	(Colchester United won 5–4 on agg)

1997/98

R1(1) Cambridge United	A 1–1
R1(2) Cambridge United	H 2–1
	(West Brom won 3–2 on agg)
R2(1) Luton Town	A 1–1
R2(2) Luton Town	H 4–2
	(West Brom won 5–3 on agg)
R3 Liverpool	H 0–2

1998/99

R1(1) Brentford	H 2–1
R1(2) Brentford	A 0–3
	(Brentford won 4–2 on agg)

1999/2000

R1(1) Halifax Town	A 0–0
R1(2) Halifax Town	H 5–1
	(West Brom won 5–1 on agg)
R2(1) Wycombe Wanderers	H 1–1
R2(2) Wycombe Wanderers	A 4–3
	(West Brom won 5–4 on agg)
R3 Fulham	H 1–2

2000/01

R1(1) Swansea City	A 0–0	
R1(2) Swansea City	H 2–1	
	(West Brom won 2–1 on agg)	
R2(1) Derby County	A 2–1	
R2(2) Derby County	H 2–4	
	(Derby County won 5–4 on agg)	

2001/02

R1	Cambridge United	A 1–1
	(West Brom won 4–3 on penalties)	
R2	Swindon Town	H 2–0
R3	Charlton Athletic	H 0–1

2002/03

R2	Wigan Athletic	A 1–3

2003/04

R1	Brentford	H 4–0
R2	Hartlepool United	A 2–1
R3	Newcastle United	A 2–1
R4	Manchester United	H 2–0
QF	Arsenal	H 0–2

2004/05

R2	Colchester United	A 1–2

2005/06

R2	Bradford City	H 4–1
R3	Fulham	A 3–2
R4	Manchester United	A 1–3

2006/07

R1	Leyton Orient	A 3–0
R2	Cheltenham Town	H 3–1
R3	Arsenal	H 0–2

2007/08

R1	Bournemouth	H 1–0
R2	Peterborough United	A 2–0
R3	Cardiff City	A 2–4

2008/09

| R2 | Hartlepool United | A 1–2 |

ASA CLUBS

One of Albion's brightest stars of the late 1960s was Scottish midfield schemer Asa Hartford. Asa played in the 1970 League Cup final defeat to Manchester City but his sparkling displays soon caught the eye of Leeds United boss Don Revie and in November 1971, Albion reluctantly accepted a bid from Leeds. The high-profile transfer to Elland Road was, however, dramatically cancelled when a suspected hole-in-the-heart condition was discovered during a routine pre-transfer medical examination.

Revie was devastated and Hartford's dream of playing in the most successful team of the era was over – many wondered if it might signal the end of his career at The Hawthorns. Of course, he proved the doubters wrong and eventually was transferred to Manchester City at a cost of £210,000 and went on to become a huge crowd favourite, winning 50 caps for Scotland in the process.

Of the Leeds United affair, in later years Asa said, 'Undoubtedly my biggest disappointment was when my transfer to Don Revie's Leeds United fell through on medical grounds due to the heart problem, which my cardiologist gave me the all-clear on. I'd dreamed of being in a midfield three that read: Bremner, Giles and Hartford, and Leeds at that time were one of the best teams in Europe and it would have been a great thrill to play for them.'

BIG RON QUOTES – VOLUME 3

More of Atko's 'Ronglish' . . . again, no explanations necessary. . . .

'I would not say that he [David Ginola] is one of the best left wingers in the Premiership, but there are none better.'

'They've come out at half time and gone bang.'

'[Phil Neville] was treading on dangerous water there. . . .'

'I've had this sneaking feeling throughout the game that it's there to be won. . . .'

'I would also think that the replay showed it to be worse than it actually was.'

'Beckenbauer has really gambled all his eggs.'

'If Glenn Hoddle said one word to his team at half time, it was concentration and focus.'

'They must go for it now as they have nothing to lose but the match.'

'I think that was a moment of cool panic there.'

'Woodcock would have scored, but his shot was too perfect.'

'Someone in the England team will have to grab the ball by the horns.'

'He's not only a good player, but he's spiteful in the nicest sense of the word.'

'Tony Adams – he's the rock that the team has grown from.'

'. . . and he [Peter Schmeichel] extends and grows even bigger than he is.'

TEXACO CUP

A forerunner to the Anglo-Scottish Cup, Albion took part in the Texaco Cup on three occasions. Morton proved too good in 1970, winning 2–1 in Scotland and 1–0 at The Hawthorns. Two years later Albion again took part in the pre-season tournament, beating Sheffield United 2–1 over two legs before Newcastle United recovered from a 2–1 first leg defeat to win the return 3–1 at St James' Park. By 1975 the format involved a group stage and the Baggies' third and final attempt resulted in a 0–0 draw with Blues, a 5–1 romp over Norwich and a 2–1 loss at Peterborough United, failing to progress.

The total record is:
1970/71
Leg 1   Morton 2–1 WBA
Leg 2   WBA 0–1 Morton

1972/73
Leg 1   Sheffield United 1–1 WBA
Leg 2   WBA 1–0 Sheffield United
R2
Leg 1   WBA 2–1 Newcastle United
Leg 2   Newcastle 3–1 WBA

1974/75
Group 1
               Birmingham City 0–0 WBA
               WBA 5–1 Norwich
               Peterborough 2–1 WBA

Pld: 9   W: 3   D: 2   L: 4   F: 12   A: 11

ANGLO-SCOTTISH CUP

The Texaco Cup competition limped on until the mid-1970s as the Anglo-Scottish Cup, but Albion never made it past the group stages in either 1975 or 1976. The tournament, dogged by poor crowds and no sponsorship, faded into obscurity.

1975/76
Anglo-Scottish Cup Group 2
WBA 1–1 Mansfield Town
Hull City 1–2 WBA
Leicester City 2–1 WBA

1976/77
Anglo-Scottish Cup Group 2
Bristol City 1–0 WBA
Nottingham Forest 3–2 WBA
WBA 3–1 Notts County

Total record:
Pld: 6   W: 2   D: 1   L: 3   F: 9   A: 9

FULL MEMBERS' CUP

The Full Members' Cup became the Simod Cup in the
1987/88 season.

Full Members 1985/86
Group 4
Brighton 1–2 WBA
WBA 2–1 Crystal Palace
SF WBA 2–2 Chelsea (Chelsea won on penalties)

Simod Cup
1987/88
R1 Oldham 0–3 WBA
R2 Ipswich Town 2–1 WBA

1988/89
R1 West Ham United 5–2 WBA

Associate Members' Cup
1991/92
Group 6 Southern
WBA 4–0 Shrewsbury Town
Lincoln City 1–2 WBA
Southern R1 WBA 0–1 Exeter City

1992/93
Group 2 Southern
WBA 4–0 Walsall
Mansfield Town 0–1 WBA
Southern R2   WBA 2–1 Torquay United
Southern QF   Stoke City 2–1 WBA

ANGLO-ITALIAN CUP

In the final attempt to make a success of a competition
starting with 'Anglo', second-tier English teams took
on second-tier Italian teams. Albion participated twice,
reaching the semis in 1995/96. Here is the total record:

1993/94
Group 4
Leicester City 0–0 WBA
WBA 3–1 Peterborough United
R1 Group 2:
WBA 1–2 Pescara (Ita)
WBA 3–4 Padova (Ita)
Fiorentina (Ita) 2–0 WBA
Cosenza (Ita) 2–1 WBA

1995/96
Group 2
Salernitana 0–0 WBA
WBA 1–2 Foggia
WBA 2–1 Reggiana
Brescia 0–1 WBA
QF Birmingham 2–2 WBA (West Brom won on penalties)
SF leg 1 WBA 0–0 Port Vale
SF leg 2 Port Vale 3–1 WBA

Total record:
Pld: 13 W: 3   D: 4   L: 6   F: 15   A: 19   GD: -4

THE BAGGIES' COMPLETE LEAGUE RECORD

		Home			Away			Totals (H&A)				
Pld	W	D	L	W	D	L	W	D	L	F	A	Pts

2008/09   1   Premiership

Pld	W	D	L	W	D	L	W	D	L	F	A	Pts
38	7	3	9	1	5	13	8	8	22	36	67	32

20th/20

2007/08   2   Championship

Pld	W	D	L	W	D	L	W	D	L	F	A	Pts
46	12	8	3	11	4	8	23	12	11	88	55	81

1st/24

2006/07   2   Championship

Pld	W	D	L	W	D	L	W	D	L	F	A	Pts
46	14	4	5	8	6	9	22	10	14	81	55	76

4th/24

2005/06   1   Premiership

Pld	W	D	L	W	D	L	W	D	L	F	A	Pts
38	6	2	11	1	7	11	7	9	22	31	58	30

19th/20

2004/05   1   Premiership

Pld	W	D	L	W	D	L	W	D	L	F	A	Pts
38	5	8	6	1	8	10	6	16	16	36	61	34

17th/20

2003/04   2   Division One

Pld	W	D	L	W	D	L	W	D	L	F	A	Pts
46	14	5	4	11	6	6	25	11	10	64	42	86

2nd/24

2002/03   1   Premiership

Pld	W	D	L	W	D	L	W	D	L	F	A	Pts
38	3	5	11	3	3	13	6	8	24	29	65	26

19th/20

	Home			Away			Totals (H&A)					
Pld	W	D	L	W	D	L	W	D	L	F	A	Pts

2001/02 2 Division One
| 46 | 15 | 4 | 4 | 12 | 4 | 7 | 27 | 8 | 11 | 61 | 29 | 89 |
2nd/24

2000/01 2 Division One
| 46 | 13 | 5 | 5 | 8 | 6 | 9 | 21 | 11 | 14 | 60 | 52 | 74 |
6th/24

1999/00 2 Division One
| 46 | 6 | 11 | 6 | 4 | 8 | 11 | 10 | 19 | 17 | 43 | 60 | 49 |
21st/24

1998/99 2 Division One
| 46 | 12 | 4 | 7 | 4 | 7 | 12 | 16 | 11 | 19 | 69 | 76 | 59 |
12th/24

1997/98 2 Division One
| 46 | 9 | 8 | 6 | 7 | 5 | 11 | 16 | 13 | 17 | 50 | 56 | 61 |
10th/24

1996/97 2 Division One
| 46 | 7 | 7 | 9 | 7 | 8 | 8 | 14 | 15 | 17 | 68 | 72 | 57 |
16th/24

1995/96 2 Division One
| 46 | 11 | 5 | 7 | 5 | 7 | 11 | 16 | 12 | 18 | 60 | 68 | 60 |
11th/24

1994/95 2 Division One
| 46 | 13 | 3 | 7 | 3 | 7 | 13 | 16 | 10 | 20 | 51 | 57 | 58 |
19th/24

	Home			Away			Totals (H&A)					
Pld	W	D	L	W	D	L	W	D	L	F	A	Pts

1993/94 2 Division One

46	9	7	7	4	5	14	13	12	21	60	69	51

21st/24

1992/93 3 Division Two

46	17	3	3	8	7	8	25	10	11	88	54	85

4th/24

1991/92 3 Division Three

46	12	6	5	7	8	8	19	14	13	64	49	71

7th/24

1990/91 2 Division Two

46	7	11	5	3	7	13	10	18	18	52	61	48

23rd/24

1989/90 2 Division Two

46	6	8	9	6	7	10	12	15	19	67	71	51

20th/24

1988/89 2 Division Two

46	13	7	3	5	11	7	18	18	10	65	41	72

9th/24

1987/88 2 Division Two

44	8	7	7	4	4	14	12	11	21	50	69	47

20th/23

1986/87 2 Division Two

42	8	6	7	5	6	10	13	12	17	51	49	51

15th/22

	Home			Away			Totals (H&A)					
Pld	W	D	L	W	D	L	W	D	L	F	A	Pts

1985/86   1   First Division

| 42 | 3 | 8 | 10 | 1 | 4 | 16 | 4 | 12 | 26 | 35 | 89 | 24 |

22nd/22

1984/85   1   First Division

| 42 | 11 | 4 | 6 | 5 | 3 | 13 | 16 | 7 | 19 | 58 | 62 | 55 |

12th/22

1983/84   1   First Division

| 42 | 10 | 4 | 7 | 4 | 5 | 12 | 14 | 9 | 19 | 48 | 62 | 51 |

17th/22

1982/83   1   First Division

| 42 | 11 | 5 | 5 | 4 | 7 | 10 | 15 | 12 | 15 | 51 | 49 | 57 |

11th/22

1981/82   1   First Division

| 42 | 6 | 6 | 9 | 5 | 5 | 11 | 11 | 11 | 20 | 46 | 57 | 44 |

17th/22

1980/81   1   First Division

| 42 | 15 | 4 | 2 | 5 | 8 | 8 | 20 | 12 | 10 | 60 | 42 | 52 |

4th/22

1979/80   1   First Division

| 42 | 9 | 8 | 4 | 2 | 11 | 8 | 11 | 19 | 12 | 54 | 50 | 41 |

10th/22

1978/79   1   First Division

| 42 | 13 | 5 | 3 | 11 | 6 | 4 | 24 | 11 | 7 | 72 | 35 | 59 |

3rd/22

	Home			Away			Totals (H&A)					
Pld	W	D	L	W	D	L	W	D	L	F	A	Pts

1977/78   1   First Division

42	13	5	3	5	9	7	18	14	10	62	53	50

6th/22

1976/77   1   First Division

42	10	6	5	6	7	8	16	13	13	62	56	45

7th/22

1975/76   2   Division Two

42	10	9	2	10	4	7	20	13	9	50	33	53

3rd/22

1974/75   2   Division Two

42	13	4	4	5	5	11	18	9	15	54	42	45

6th/22

1973/74   2   Division Two

42	8	9	4	6	7	8	14	16	12	48	45	44

8th/22

1972/73   1   First Division

42	8	7	6	1	3	17	9	10	23	38	62	28

22nd/22

1971/72   1   First Division

42	6	7	8	6	4	11	12	11	19	42	54	35

16th/22

1970/71   1   First Division

42	9	8	4	1	7	13	10	15	17	58	75	35

17th/22

	Home			Away			Totals (H&A)					
Pld	W	D	L	W	D	L	W	D	L	F	A	Pts

1969/70   1   First Division

| 42 | 10 | 6 | 5 | 4 | 3 | 14 | 14 | 9 | 19 | 58 | 66 | 37 |

16th/22

1968/69   1   First Division

| 42 | 11 | 7 | 3 | 5 | 4 | 12 | 16 | 11 | 15 | 64 | 67 | 43 |

10th/22

1967/68   1   First Division

| 42 | 12 | 4 | 5 | 5 | 8 | 8 | 17 | 12 | 13 | 75 | 62 | 46 |

8th/22

1966/67   1   First Division

| 42 | 11 | 1 | 9 | 5 | 6 | 10 | 16 | 7 | 19 | 77 | 73 | 39 |

13th/22

1965/66   1   First Division

| 42 | 11 | 6 | 4 | 8 | 6 | 7 | 19 | 12 | 11 | 91 | 69 | 50 |

6th/22

1964/65   1   First Division

| 42 | 10 | 5 | 6 | 3 | 8 | 10 | 13 | 13 | 16 | 70 | 65 | 39 |

14th/22

1963/64   1   First Division

| 42 | 9 | 6 | 6 | 7 | 5 | 9 | 16 | 11 | 15 | 70 | 61 | 43 |

10th/22

1962/63   1   First Division

| 42 | 11 | 1 | 9 | 5 | 6 | 10 | 16 | 7 | 19 | 71 | 79 | 39 |

14th/22

Pld	Home W	D	L	Away W	D	L	Totals (H&A) W	D	L	F	A	Pts

1961/62   1   First Division

| 42 | 10 | 7 | 4 | 5 | 6 | 10 | 15 | 13 | 14 | 83 | 67 | 43 |

9th/22

1960/61   1   First Division

| 42 | 10 | 3 | 8 | 8 | 2 | 11 | 18 | 5 | 19 | 67 | 71 | 41 |

10th/22

1959/60   1   First Division

| 42 | 12 | 4 | 5 | 7 | 7 | 7 | 19 | 11 | 12 | 83 | 57 | 49 |

4th/22

1958/59   1   First Division

| 42 | 8 | 7 | 6 | 10 | 6 | 5 | 18 | 13 | 11 | 88 | 68 | 49 |

5th/22

1957/58   1   First Division

| 42 | 14 | 4 | 3 | 4 | 10 | 7 | 18 | 14 | 10 | 92 | 70 | 50 |

4th/22

1956/57   1   First Division

| 42 | 8 | 8 | 5 | 6 | 6 | 9 | 14 | 14 | 14 | 59 | 61 | 42 |

11th/22

1955/56   1   First Division

| 42 | 13 | 3 | 5 | 5 | 2 | 14 | 18 | 5 | 19 | 58 | 70 | 41 |

13th/22

1954/55   1   First Division

| 42 | 11 | 5 | 5 | 5 | 3 | 13 | 16 | 8 | 18 | 76 | 96 | 40 |

17th/22

	Home			Away			Totals (H&A)					
Pld	W	D	L	W	D	L	W	D	L	F	A	Pts

1953/54   1   First Division

	Home			Away			Totals (H&A)					
42	13	5	3	9	4	8	22	9	11	86	63	53

2nd/22

1952/53   1   First Division

42	13	3	5	8	5	8	21	8	13	66	60	50

4th/22

1951/52   1   First Division

42	8	9	4	6	4	11	14	13	15	74	77	41

13th/22

1950/51   1   First Division

42	7	4	10	6	7	8	13	11	18	53	61	37

16th/22

1949/50   1   First Division

42	9	7	5	5	5	11	14	12	16	47	53	40

14th/22

1948/49   2   Division Two

42	16	3	2	8	5	8	24	8	10	69	39	56

2nd/22

1947/48   2   Division Two

42	11	4	6	7	5	9	18	9	15	63	58	45

7th/22

1946/47   2   Division Two

42	12	4	5	8	4	9	20	8	14	88	75	48

7th/22

	Home			Away			Totals (H&A)					
Pld	W	D	L	W	D	L	W	D	L	F	A	Pts

1939/40   2   Division Two
Play suspended after three games until 1946 due to war

1938/39   2   Division Two

Pld	W	D	L	W	D	L	W	D	L	F	A	Pts
42	15	3	3	3	6	12	18	9	15	89	72	45

10th/22

1937/38   1   First Division

Pld	W	D	L	W	D	L	W	D	L	F	A	Pts
42	10	5	6	4	3	14	14	8	20	74	91	36

22nd/22

1936/37   1   First Division

Pld	W	D	L	W	D	L	W	D	L	F	A	Pts
42	13	3	5	3	3	15	16	6	20	77	98	38

16th/22

1935/36   1   First Division

Pld	W	D	L	W	D	L	W	D	L	F	A	Pts
42	12	3	6	4	3	14	16	6	20	89	88	38

18th/22

1934/35   1   First Division

Pld	W	D	L	W	D	L	W	D	L	F	A	Pts
42	10	8	3	7	2	12	17	10	15	83	83	44

9th/22

1933/34   1   First Division

Pld	W	D	L	W	D	L	W	D	L	F	A	Pts
42	12	4	5	5	6	10	17	10	15	78	70	44

7th/22

1932/33   1   First Division

Pld	W	D	L	W	D	L	W	D	L	F	A	Pts
42	16	1	4	4	8	9	20	9	13	83	70	49

4th/22

	Home			Away			Totals (H&A)					
Pld	W	D	L	W	D	L	W	D	L	F	A	Pts

1931/32   1   First Division

42	12	4	5	8	2	11	20	6	16	77	55	46

6th/22

1930/31   2   Division Two

42	14	3	4	8	7	6	22	10	10	83	49	54

2nd/22

1929/30   2   Division Two

42	16	1	4	5	4	12	21	5	16	105	73	47

6th/22

1928/29   2   Division Two

42	13	4	4	6	4	11	19	8	15	80	79	46

7th/22

1927/28   2   Division Two

42	10	7	4	7	5	9	17	12	13	90	70	46

8th/22

1926/27   1   First Division

42	10	4	7	1	4	16	11	8	23	65	86	30

22nd/22

1925/26   1   First Division

42	13	5	3	3	3	15	16	8	18	79	78	40

13th/22

1924/25   1   First Division

42	13	6	2	10	4	7	23	10	9	58	34	56

2nd/22

| | Home | | | Away | | | Totals (H&A) | | | | | |
| Pld | W | D | L | W | D | L | W | D | L | F | A | Pts |

1923/24 1 First Division

| 42 | 10 | 6 | 5 | 2 | 8 | 11 | 12 | 14 | 16 | 51 | 62 | 38 |

16th/22

1922/23 1 First Division

| 42 | 12 | 7 | 2 | 5 | 4 | 12 | 17 | 11 | 14 | 58 | 49 | 45 |

7th/22

1921/22 1 First Division

| 42 | 8 | 6 | 7 | 7 | 4 | 10 | 15 | 10 | 17 | 51 | 63 | 40 |

13th/22

1920/21 1 First Division

| 42 | 8 | 7 | 6 | 5 | 7 | 9 | 13 | 14 | 15 | 54 | 58 | 40 |

14th/22

1919/20 1 First Division

| 42 | 17 | 1 | 3 | 11 | 3 | 7 | 28 | 4 | 10 | 104 | 47 | 60 |

1st/22

No league football from 1915/16 to 1918/19 (due to war)

1914/15 1 First Division

| 38 | 11 | 5 | 3 | 4 | 5 | 10 | 15 | 10 | 13 | 49 | 43 | 40 |

10th/20

1913/14 1 First Division

| 38 | 11 | 7 | 1 | 4 | 6 | 9 | 15 | 13 | 10 | 46 | 42 | 43 |

5th/20

		Home			Away			Totals (H&A)					
	Pld	W	D	L	W	D	L	W	D	L	F	A	Pts

1912/13 — First Division
38	8	7	4	5	5	9	13	12	13	57	50	38
10th/20

1911/12 — First Division
38	10	6	3	5	3	11	15	9	14	43	47	39
9th/20

1910/11 — Division Two
38	14	2	3	8	7	4	22	9	7	67	41	53
1st/20

1909/10 — Division Two
38	8	5	6	8	0	11	16	5	17	58	56	37
11th/20

1908/09 — Division Two
38	13	5	1	6	8	5	19	13	6	56	27	51
3rd/20

1907/08 — Division Two
38	13	3	3	6	6	7	19	9	10	61	39	47
5th/20

1906/07 — Division Two
38	15	2	2	6	3	10	21	5	12	83	45	47
4th/20

1905/06 — Division Two
38	13	4	2	9	4	6	22	8	8	79	36	52
4th/20

	Home			Away			Totals (H&A)					
Pld	W	D	L	W	D	L	W	D	L	F	A	Pts

1904/05   2   Division Two

Pld	W	D	L	W	D	L	W	D	L	F	A	Pts
34	8	2	7	5	2	10	13	4	17	56	48	30

10th/18

1903/04   1   First Division

Pld	W	D	L	W	D	L	W	D	L	F	A	Pts
34	4	8	5	3	2	12	7	10	17	36	60	24

18th/18

1902/03   1   First Division

Pld	W	D	L	W	D	L	W	D	L	F	A	Pts
34	10	2	5	6	2	9	16	4	14	54	53	36

7th/18

1901/02   2   Division Two

Pld	W	D	L	W	D	L	W	D	L	F	A	Pts
34	14	2	1	11	3	3	25	5	4	82	29	55

1st/18

1900/01   1   First Division

Pld	W	D	L	W	D	L	W	D	L	F	A	Pts
34	4	4	9	3	4	10	7	8	19	35	62	22

18th/18

1899/1900   1   First Division

Pld	W	D	L	W	D	L	W	D	L	F	A	Pts
34	8	6	3	3	2	12	11	8	15	43	51	30

13th/18

1898/99   1   First Division

Pld	W	D	L	W	D	L	W	D	L	F	A	Pts
34	11	1	5	1	5	11	12	6	16	42	57	30

14th/18

1897/98   1   First Division

Pld	W	D	L	W	D	L	W	D	L	F	A	Pts
30	8	5	2	3	5	7	11	10	9	44	45	32

7th/16

| | Home | | | Away | | | Totals (H&A) | | | | | |
Pld	W	D	L	W	D	L	W	D	L	F	A	Pts

1896/97   1   First Division

| 30 | 7 | 2 | 6 | 3 | 4 | 8 | 10 | 6 | 14 | 33 | 56 | 26 |

12th/16

1895/96   1   First Division

| 30 | 5 | 4 | 6 | 1 | 3 | 11 | 6 | 7 | 17 | 30 | 59 | 19 |

16th/16

1894/95   1   First Division

| 30 | 9 | 2 | 4 | 1 | 2 | 12 | 10 | 4 | 16 | 51 | 66 | 24 |

13th/16

1893/94   1   First Division

| 30 | 8 | 4 | 3 | 6 | 0 | 9 | 14 | 4 | 12 | 66 | 59 | 32 |

8th/16

1892/93   1   First Division

| 30 | 9 | 2 | 4 | 3 | 3 | 9 | 12 | 5 | 13 | 58 | 69 | 29 |

8th/16

1891/92   1   Football Lg

| 26 | 6 | 3 | 4 | 0 | 3 | 10 | 6 | 6 | 14 | 51 | 58 | 18 |

12th/14

1890/91   1   Football Lg

| 22 | 3 | 1 | 7 | 2 | 1 | 8 | 5 | 2 | 15 | 34 | 57 | 12 |

12th/12

1889/90   1   Football Lg

| 22 | 8 | 1 | 2 | 3 | 2 | 6 | 11 | 3 | 8 | 47 | 50 | 25 |

5th/12

	Home			Away			Totals (H&A)					
Pld	W	D	L	W	D	L	W	D	L	F	A	Pts

1888/89   1   Football Lg

22	6	2	3	4	0	7	10	2	10	40	46	22

6th/12

WEST BROMWICH ALBION FC
ROLL OF HONOUR

FA Cup Winners: 1888, 1892, 1931, 1954, 1968

FA Cup runners-up: 1886, 1887, 1895, 1912, 1935

League Cup Winners: 1966

League Cup runners-up: 1967, 1970

League Division One (old) Champions: 1920

The Championship Champions: 2008

League Division One (old) runners-up: 1925, 1954

League Division One runners-up: 2002, 2004

League Division Two Champions: 1902, 1911

League Division Two runners-up: 1931, 1949

League Division Three play-off winners: 1993

Record Attendance: 64,815 v Arsenal
(FA Cup 6th round 6 March 1937)

Record Win: 12–0 v Darwen, 1892

Record Defeat: 3–10 v Stoke City, 1937

THE GAFFERS

Albion's manager's office, it's oft been said, has a revolving door on it with the West Brom board not afraid to hire and fire at will. Here are the brave souls who've attempted to bring the club success over the years. . . .

Louis Ford (1890–92)
The first secretary-manager of the club, within his spell in charge he oversaw the FA Cup triumph in 1892. Ford also had a variety of other roles in football, including being a FA Councillor, vice-president of the Football League, secretary of Walsall and Leicester and even a referee – busy guy!

Henry Jackson (1892–94)
Jackson was a member of the board who was appointed to the role of secretary-manager while still fulfilling his board room commitments. He later took on a similar role at Leicester Fosse – in other words, he was the boss of the Fosse.

Edward Stephenson (1894–95)
Stephenson endured a short time in charge until his superiors realised he was not up to the job and was subsequently sacked for incompetence. This could be seen as slightly harsh as he did manage to get the team to the FA Cup final that season. If only the board had realised what real incompetence was. . . .

Clement Keys (1895–96)

He may sound like a harbour named after the marauding fullback Neil, but Clement Keys was only at the club for a year, and in that time achieved nigh-on nothing and was replaced.

Frank Heaven (1896–1902)

Heaven acted as secretary, manager and financial secretary at the club. During his tenure he won the Second Division in 1902, but then due to a disagreement with the board was forced to resign from his various positions. Heaven was also a key figure in the overseeing of the club's move to their new stadium – The Hawthorns – in 1900; so in many respects, the Baggies' home really was heaven sent!

Fred Everiss (1902–48)

Theoretically, Everiss is the longest-serving manager in the history of English football. However, this title is slightly debatable due to the fact that while he was the manager of the team, his job description was far different from that of the modern gaffer. He never actually picked the team – the club's directors undertook this task. The majority of Everiss' role was administrative, as he also operated as the club secretary. Everiss eventually moved 'upstairs' in 1948 in order to become a director, and the position of 'manager' was created as a single occupation. During his time as manager he guided Albion to their one and only First Division title in 1920 and the FA Cup in 1931 and, therefore, is the most successful boss the club has ever had.

Jack Smith (1948–52)

The club's first official manager, Smith took West Brom up to the First Division. His most famous signing for the club, for a then record fee of £20,000, was Ronnie Allen who arrived from Port Vale.

Jesse Carver (1952–53)

Carver was one of many to have their career cut short by the Second World War and prior to the conflict he had played for Newcastle. His journey to The Hawthorns took in stints in Holland, and winning Serie A with Juventus. Carver was the first manager to bring the idea of football coaching into training sessions instead of just aiming to have the players as fit as possible. However, after only eight months in charge he returned to Italy to coach Lazio. From this point on he became an international journeyman, moving around Italy and then taking in periods in Cyprus, and a short stay with the less exotic Coventry City.

Vic Buckingham (1953–59)

Buckingham was a one-club man who spent a decade of his playing career with Tottenham, including the war period. He arrived at The Albion via Bradford Park Avenue and brought with him the idea of quality, passing football. In 1954 he almost got the club to win the Holy Grail of English football – the League and FA Cup double – but fell short by only finishing second in the First Division. He did, however, secure the FA Cup. Coveted around Europe, it was five years before he was lured away from the club, with Dutch giants Ajax proving to be too tempting a proposition. He was one of the first people to spot a young Johan Cruyff and helped formulate the Ajax youth system. Buckingham returned to English football for a year in 1963, but quickly left after being involved in a betting scandal while managing Sheffield Wednesday, and went back to Amsterdam. He then had time in charge at both Sevilla and Barcelona, before ending his managerial career in Greece with Olympiakos.

Gordon Clark (1959–61)

During his two years at West Brom, Clark failed to achieve anything of note and is therefore barely remembered in the history of the club. He did, however, continue to build on the attractive passing game his predecessor had ingrained in the hearts and minds of the Albion faithful, though it was not productive enough to win trophies.

Archie Macauley (1961–63)

A wing-half by trade, he started his career at Glasgow Rangers before moving south of the border to play for several London clubs including West Ham and Arsenal. He dropped down from the top division to take the player-manager role at Guildford, where he cut his teeth as a coach. In 1959, he famously took Norwich of the Third Division to the FA Cup semi-finals. However, at West Brom he achieved little more than mid-table mediocrity and left after two seasons in the top job. Macauley's final job in management came at Brighton where he stayed until 1968.

Jimmy Hagan (1963–67)

Hagan spent the majority of his career at Sheffield United before going into management. In his first role as a manager, he took Peterborough into the Football League for the first time in their history and then won the Division Four title. These successes enhanced his reputation in the game and the Baggies quickly snapped him up. At The Hawthorns his magical touch continued and the League Cup was brought back to the Midlands in 1966. Even with this level of achievement, the board deemed it necessary to dispense with his services only a year later. From West Bromwich he moved to Lisbon and had great success with the city's two main clubs, Sporting and Benfica. He stayed in Portugal until 1981 where he had his last managerial role with Belenenses.

Alan Ashman (1967–71)
The centre-forward had his career hit by the outbreak of war and so never got the chance to fulfil his potential. He had a successful start to his managerial career by guiding Carlisle to two successive promotions and a third-place finish in Division Two. At The Hawthorns he guided the side to FA Cup glory in 1968. This set his own downfall, as the club then failed to match these heights again and Ashman was sacked in 1971. He went on to have a spell in Greece, before returning to Carlisle for another brief period.

Don Howe (1971–75)
The full-back made almost 350 appearances for the Baggies before moving onto Arsenal, two of the clubs that he would later manage. He replaced Ashman in 1971, but under his reign Albion were relegated to the Second Division. His exit in 1975 seemed to be hastened by the departure of club legend Jeff Astle, and Jonny Giles subsequently replaced him. He has had a wide ranging career since then, managing Arsenal and taking on a variety of roles with England over a 20-year period. He retired in 2003 and now intermittently works as a pundit.

Jonny Giles (1975–77 and 1984–85)

The Irishman enjoyed a great playing career with Manchester United, Leeds and on the international stage. As a midfielder he won a plethora of trophies including the League and FA Cup. By the time he arrived at The Hawthorns he was already the Ireland manager, while still turning out on the pitch too. He had a positive effect on the West Brom side, by getting them promoted back to the First Division and then reaching seventh the following campaign in the top flight. After two seasons in charge, he left for his homeland in order to manage Shamrock Rovers. Giles returned to the Midlands in 1984, and achieved relative success by keeping West Brom in the division and then a mid-table finish the following season. After a poor start in 1985 he was sacked. He still works in the Irish media as a pundit, but is the unfortunate owner of a rhyming name that is constantly associated with haemorrhoids!

Ronnie Allen (1977 and 1981–82)

The man from Stoke-on-Trent is quite rightly regarded as one of West Brom's greatest ever players. The short striker scored at a rate of better than one in every two games, and will be remembered for scoring twice in the FA Cup final win in 1954. As a manager he had a more varied career. Having started off at Wolves he then moved on to the Basque Country in order to work for Athletic Bilbao. He later had spells at Sporting Lisbon and Walsall before being brought back to his spiritual home; he was appointed as manager of Albion in 1977, but could not last out a year. Allen returned for another stint as manager in 1981, but again he struggled and quit after one season. He will be most fondly remembered as being the man that spotted Cyrille Regis and brought him to the club – quite a legacy. During the club's 125th anniversary celebrations he was voted as one of West Brom's best 16 players of all time. He died in 2001.

Ron Atkinson (1978–81 and 1987–88)

As a player 'Big Ron' failed to reach great heights, but quickly showed that he was an astute manager. He had a promising start at Kettering and then Cambridge United before arriving, larger than life, at The Hawthorns. Atkinson made his mark by teaming up Cyrille Regis, Brendan Batson and Laurie Cunningham – three black players whose impact was colossal – and Albion finished in third place in the top flight in 1979. Continued success brought bigger clubs searching for his services and Atkinson, AKA 'Mr Bojangles', eventually left to take charge of Manchester United.

After five years at Old Trafford he returned to the Baggies, but only for one more season. He quickly turned around the club's fortunes, but was unwilling to pass up the opportunity to move on again, this time to Spain, in order to manage Atlético Madrid. From then on he has had short spells at a variety of clubs and differing roles as a TV pundit and trouble-shooting advisor for several lower league clubs during a Sky documentary series.

Ron Wylie (1982–84)

Wylie was an experienced player, having spent many years at Notts County, Aston Villa and finally the Blues. He enjoyed a couple of coaching roles prior to taking on the job of manager with the Baggies. Wylie arrived at a difficult time for the club as many of their big-name players had been sold and the team was in a transition period. After a positive start to his time at The Hawthorns, things soon started to go wrong and after

18 months in charge he was shown the door. Following his departure he moved back to Aston Villa as reserve team manager and later a scout.

Nobby Stiles (1985–86)

Stiles achieved cult status as a player with his non-stereotypical appearance and his fearless attitude on the pitch. He was a member of the 1966 World Cup-winning side, and the victorious Manchester United team from the 1968 European Cup. Like many top players he struggled to adapt to management. For his first role, he took over from his former team-mate Bobby Charlton at Preston North End. This was to be followed by a stint in the NASL where he worked for the Vancouver Wildcats. The Baggies gave him the opportunity to return to English football, but his time at the club was disappointing and in six months at the helm, he was only able to oversee three victories. His last position in the game was as coach of the Manchester United youth team that included Beckham, Scholes and many others.

Ron Saunders (1986–87)

A formidable lower-league striker, Saunders went into management with Yeovil Town following his retirement. Following a spell as Norwich boss where he progressed quickly, he became Manchester City manager and took them to the League Cup final where they lost 2–1 to Wolves. Saunders then had eight years at Aston Villa in which he turned them into one of the strongest sides in English football, subsequently winning the First Division title. West Brom was to be Saunders' last role in management, as he took them down to the Second Division, and then he failed to regain their top-flight status the next season and was relieved of his duties.

His association with the Dark Side (the Villa) was never going to win him too many popularity contests, it has to be said.

Brian Talbot (1988–91)
Talbot was appointed player-manager in 1988. Talbot started off brightly at the club, and got the side in and around the play-offs in his first season. However, after failing to gain promotion, the side started to slide the following season and continued in this vain for the next campaign, too. Following his dismissal he went on to manage in Malta on two separate occasions, but had his most successful time at Rushden & Diamonds, taking them from the Conference to Division Two.

Bobby Gould (1991–92)
The former Baggies player arrived back at The Hawthorns in 1991 with the mandate of trying to stop them from dropping into the Third Division. Alas, he failed with the first task and then also did not manage to get them back up into the Second Division. This cost the colourful Englishman his job. Later in his career he managed Wales. He will always be best remembered for masterminding Wimbledon's shock 1–0 FA Cup final victory over Liverpool in 1988.

Ossie Ardiles (1992–93)
Ardiles made his name in England with Spurs. Although he was undoubtedly a great player, he was unable to take any of this success into management and has had 14 managerial roles in 20 years, rarely enjoying sustained success with any one club. At West Brom he did take the team up to the Second Division following a play-off

final victory over Port Vale. This success saw Tottenham asking for his services and Ardiles returned to his cultural home.

Keith Burkinshaw (1993–94)
Burkinshaw had a reasonably average career as a player. However, as a manager he has been all over the world, from Portugal to Bahrain. Originally the assistant to Ardiles, he was given the top job after the Argentinian left for Tottenham in 1993. Burkinshaw was unable to form a cohesive side and managed only one season at the helm, in which the Baggies only just avoided relegation.

Alan Buckley (1994–97)
A former Walsall player and manager, the man from the Saddlers had three years at WBA. His time at The Hawthorns was sandwiched in between spells at Grimsby. Like many other gaffers, Buckley was unable to create a top Division One side and paid the price by losing his job in 1997.

Ray Harford (1997)
The former Blackburn manager took up the challenge of keeping WBA in the First Division, and subsequently succeeded. Unfortunately, the following season was a disappointment and this, coupled with Harford's increasing annoyance at driving 100 miles from his home to West Bromwich, led to his departure The next two teams to make it onto Harford's CV were QPR and Millwall. Sadly, he died at the age of 58 having suffered from lung cancer while still working at The Den.

Denis Smith (1997–99)

Smith enjoyed an average spell in charge at The Hawthorns having achieved only mid-table finishes for two seasons on the trot and was subsequently sacked. He spent the majority of his playing career at Stoke, where he made almost 500 appearances. Smith's most successful time as a manager was at Wrexham, where he was at the helm for five years. At least he ended the Stoke City hoodoo – well, for one game!

Brian Little (1999–2000)

Little arrived with a good reputation that even survived a poor spell at Stoke. He had managerial experience in the Premier League with Aston Villa, where he had played most of his career. At The Hawthorns he was told to get them back into the top flight, but failed and left the club languishing in the lower reaches of the First Division. Further jobs came his way, but he never reached the heights he had enjoyed at Aston Villa, and his most recent role was at Wrexham, whom he left in 2008 while they were in the Blue Square Premier.

Gary Megson (2000–04)

Coincidentally, Megson also replaced Brian Little at Stoke. He only managed a few months at the Britannia Stadium, not due to any fault of his own with his departure caused by the club being taken over by an Icelandic consortium who wanted to bring in their own man. At Albion he kept the club up on the last day with a win, only a month after starting the role. This relative success gave the side momentum that was taken into the following season, in which they reached the play-off semi-finals only to be defeated by Bolton. In 2002 he took the club back to the Premier League but then Megson had a number of fallings-out with both Paul Thompson and his replacement as Chairman, Jeremy Peace, about the direction he felt the club was heading in. In 2004, despite regaining top-flight status for a second time for the club, he left for pastures new. He currently manages Bolton Wanderers in the Premier League.

Bryan Robson (2004–06)

The Manchester United and England legend returned to his first club, and was given the nigh-on impossible task of keeping WBA up from the precarious position of being bottom at Christmas. However, after some sensible transfer dealings and a dramatic set of results on the last day of the season, the Baggies sensationally avoided the drop. Sadly, this success did not continue and the side was relegated the following year. After an average start in the Championship, Robson left the club. Since leaving the Baggies he has worked at Sheffield United, where he had a disappointing spell, and has since been an ambassador for Manchester United.

Tony Mowbray (2006–09)

Since becoming a manager, Mowbray has been praised for the way his sides play purist football. Mowbray had his first taste of management in a caretaker capacity at Ipswich Town, before taking his first full-time role in Scotland at Hibernian. After two seasons of relative success in Edinburgh, Mowbray was lured to England, mainly due to the prospect of managing in the Premier League – if he could guide the Baggies to the Promised Land. He achieved this in 2008, but was unable to keep the side up the following season. At the end of the 2008/09 campaign the man from Teesside disappointed his legion of Baggies admirers by leaving to manage his former club Celtic.

Roberto Di Matteo (2009–)

The former Italian international had minimal managerial experience prior to arriving at The Hawthorns, having only had one season as boss at MK Dons. As a player, he spent five years playing in Switzerland, the country where he was born, before moving to Italian giants Lazio. To the English, he is most well known for his time at Chelsea. In West London he won a host of cup competitions, including the European Cup Winners' Cup and the FA Cup on two occasions, famously scoring after just 43 seconds against Middlesbrough in one particular match. His mandate is to keep the Mowbray style, add a touch of steel, and steer this great club back to where it belongs.

BAGGIES v WOLVES – THE COMPLETE HISTORY

Here are a few of Albion's more memorable tussles with Wolves over the years, starting with a couple of salient facts:

Albion played Wolves 5 times in the 2006/07 season. In Tony Mowbray's first game as West Brom manager, they beat Wolves 3–0 at The Hawthorns. They lost the return fixture at Molineux but did knock Wolves out of the FA Cup and beat them over two legs in the Championship play-off semi-finals.

2006/07   22 October   West Brom 3–0 Wolves
Championship

2006/07   28 January   Wolves 0–3 West Brom
FA Cup

2006/07   11 March   Wolves 1–0 West Brom
Championship

2006/07   13 May   Wolves 2–3 West Brom
Championship play-off semi-final first leg

2006/07   16 May   West Brom 1–0 Wolves
Championship play-off semi-final second leg

Albion had a 7 match unbeaten record against Wolves between 1997 and 2000. They won 4 times and drew 3.

1997/98   24 August   West Brom 1–0 Wolves
League Division One

1997/98   31 January   Wolves 0–1 West Brom
League Division One

1998/99   29 November   West Brom 2–0 Wolves
League Division One

1998/99   25 April   Wolves 1–1 West Brom
League Division One

1999/2000   3 October   Wolves 1–1 West Brom
League Division One

1999/2000   31 October   West Brom 1–1 Wolves
League Division One

2000/01   17 October   West Brom 1–0 Wolves
League Division One

In 1961/62 Albion knocked Wolves out of the FA Cup and had an excellent 5–1 victory at Molineux in the League. However, the following season Wolves exacted revenge with a 7–0 thumping, the most the Baggies have ever lost to Wolves by.

1961/62 FA Cup	27 January	Wolves 1–2 West Brom
1961/62 First Division	28 March	Wolves 1–5 West Brom
1962/63 First Division	16 March	Wolves 7–0 West Brom

Between 1959 and 1961, West Brom lost 4 League encounters on the trot with Wolves, scoring 6 and conceding 12.

1959/60 First Division	5 December	West Brom 0–1 Wolves
1958/59 First Division	21 March	Wolves 5–2 West Brom
1959/60 First Division	27 February	Wolves 3–1 West Brom
1960/61 First Division	28 January	Wolves 4–2 West Brom

In 1954, Wolves and Albion shared the Charity Shield after a 4–4 draw. Ronnie Allen scored a hat trick for the Baggies. Each club would get to keep the trophy for 6 months.

1954/55   29 September   Wolves 4–4 West Brom
Charity Shield

Between 1929 and 1934, the Baggies went 11 games without losing to Wolves. They won 8 and drew 3, scoring 30 goals and conceding 13.

1928/29   23 March   Wolves 0–1 West Brom
Second Division

1929/30   31 August   Wolves 2–4 West Brom
Second Division

1929/30   28 December   West Brom 7–3 Wolves
Second Division

1930/31   11 October   West Brom 2–1 Wolves
Second Division

1930/31   18 February   Wolves 1–4 West Brom
Second Division

1930/31   28 February   West Brom 1–1 Wolves
FA Cup

1930/31   4 March   Wolves 1–2 West Brom
FA Cup

1932/33   8 October   West Brom 4–1 Wolves
First Division

1932/33   18 February   Wolves 3–3 West Brom
First Division

1933/34   7 October   Wolves 0–0 West Brom
First Division

1933/34   17 February   West Brom 2–0 Wolves
First Division

In 1893, Albion recorded their most emphatic victory over Wolves, winning 8–0 at Molineux.

1893/94   27 December   Wolves 0–8 West Brom
First Division

The first time Albion met Wolves in a competitive match was in the 1885/86 FA Cup 4th round. They won 3–1.

1885/86   2 January   West Brom 3–1 Wolves
FA Cup

The total summary of one of the oldest derby games in the history of English football is:
Played: (all comps) 156
Albion: 62 wins
Wolves: 52 wins
Draws: 42
Albion: 245 goals
Wolves: 235 goals

BAGGIES v VILLA – THE COMPLETE HISTORY

And here are some of the most memorable meetings with Villa.

Albion haven't beaten Aston Villa in their last 16 games; their last win was in 1985 and they've drawn 6 and lost 10 since then. However, they did achieve two creditable draws in the 2004/05 Premier League.

1984/85 First Division	8 April	West Brom 1–0 Aston Villa
1985/86 First Division	4 September	West Brom 0–3 Aston Villa
1985/86 League Cup	19 November	Aston Villa 2–2 West Brom
1985/86 League Cup	26 November	West Brom 1–2 Aston Villa
1985/86 First Division	28 December	Aston Villa 1–1 West Brom
1987/88 Second Division	16 September	West Brom 0–2 Aston Villa
1987/88 Second Division	18 December	Aston Villa 0–0 West Brom
1989/1990 FA Cup	17 February	West Brom 0–2 Aston Villa
1997/98 FA Cup	24 January	Aston Villa 4–0 West Brom
2002/03 Premiership	16 November	West Brom 0–0 Aston Villa
2002/03 Premiership	14 December	Aston Villa 2–1 West Brom
2004/05 Premiership	22 August	West Brom 1–1 Aston Villa

2004/05   10 April   Aston Villa 1–1 West Brom
Premiership

2005/06   2 January   West Brom 1–2 Aston Villa
Premiership

2005/06   9 April   Aston Villa 0–0 West Brom
Premiership

2008/09   21 September   West Brom 1–2 Aston Villa
Premier League

2008/09   10 January   Aston Villa 2–1 West Brom
Premier League

The Baggies lost only once in this fixture between 1964 and 1974. They beat Villa 9 times and drew twice in 12 games. One win was an emphatic 6–1 in the second round of the League Cup at The Hawthorns.

1964/65   17 October   Aston Villa 0–1 West Brom
First Division

1964/65   27 February   West Brom 3–1 Aston Villa
First Division

1965/66   16 October   Aston Villa 1–1 West Brom
First Division

1965/66   17 November   West Brom 3–1 Aston Villa
League Cup

1965/66   11 February   West Brom 2–2 Aston Villa
First Division

1966/67   14 September   West Brom 6–1 Aston Villa
League Cup

1966/67   15 October   West Brom 2–1 Aston Villa
First Division

1966/67   5 November   Aston Villa 3–2 West Brom
First Division

1969/70   3 September   Aston Villa 1–2 West Brom
League Cup

1973/74   26 December   West Brom 2–0 Aston Villa
Second Division

1973/74   2 March   Aston Villa 1–3 West Brom
Second Division

1974/75   21 December   West Brom 2–0 Aston Villa
Second Division

An impressive 27 goals were scored in just 5 matches
between 1933 and 1935. There were 3 wins for Albion
and 2 draws, one of which was a 4–4 thriller at Villa Park.
Most impressively, the Baggies thumped Villa 7–0 away,
our record score against Villa.

1933/34   16 December   West Brom 2–1 Aston Villa
First Division

1933/34   28 April   Aston Villa 4–4 West Brom
First Division

1934/35   3 November   West Brom 2–2 Aston Villa
First Division

1934/35   3 April   Aston Villa 2–3 West Brom
First Division

1935/36   19 October   Aston Villa 0–7 West Brom
First Division

Albion have played Aston Villa in 3 FA Cup finals. The
Baggies won 1, in the 1891/92 season.

1886/87   2 April   Aston Villa 2–0 West Brom
FA Cup (The Oval)

1891/92   19 March   West Brom 3–0 Aston Villa
FA Cup (The Oval)

1894/95   20 April   Aston Villa 1–0 West Brom
FA Cup (The Crystal Palace)

The total summary of the Albion–Villa derby games is:

Played: (all comps) 154
Albion: 50 wins
Villa: 73 wins
Draws: 31
Albion: 209 goals
Villa: 245 goals

RECORD TRANSFERS (IN)

£4,700,000 for Borja Valero from Real Mallorca (2008)
£3,625,000 for Robert Earnshaw from Cardiff City (2004)
£2,700,000 for Martin Albrechtsen from FC Copenhagen
     (2004)
£2,500,000 for Lee Hughes from Coventry City (2002)

£2,250,000 for Jason Koumas from Tranmere Rovers (2002)

£2,000,000 for Sean Gregan from Preston North End (2002)

£2,000,000 for Jason Roberts from Bristol Rovers (2000)

£1,250,000 for Kevin Kilbane from Preston North End (1997)

£748,000 for Peter Barnes from Manchester City (1979)

RECORD TRANSFERS (OUT)

£10,000,000 for Curtis Davies to Aston Villa (2008)

£6,000,000 for Diomansy Kamara to Fulham (2007)

£5,000,001 for Lee Hughes to Coventry City (2001)

£4,500,000 for Enzo Maresca to Juventus (2000)

IN A NUTSHELL –
THE BAGGIES' POTTED HISTORY . . .

1879 – West Bromwich Strollers are founded by a group of workers from the George Salter Spring Works on 20 September 1879.

1879 – West Bromwich Strollers play their first game with Harry Aston believed to be the club's first scorer in a 1–0 win over Black Lake Victoria at Dartmouth Park on 13 December.

1880 – The Strollers change their name to West Bromwich Albion.

1883 – Albion win their first trophy, lifting the Staffordshire Cup after beating Stoke 3–2 in the final.

1886 – The Baggies reach the FA Cup final, losing 2–0 to Blackburn Rovers.

1887 – Albion reach the FA Cup final again, but lose 2–0 to rivals Aston Villa.

1888 – It's third time lucky for Albion as they reach a third successive FA Cup final and beat Preston North End 2–1 to really put the club on the map.

1888 – The ambitiously-named World Cup sees Albion take on the Scottish FA Cup winners Renton at Hampden Park – the Scots won 4–1.

1888 – West Brom becomes one of the 12 founder members of the Football League – the very first League game sees Albion triumph 2–0 at Stoke.

1889 – West Brom reach the semi-final of the FA Cup.

1891 – They again reach the semi-final of the FA Cup.

1892 – Albion reach the FA Cup final for the fourth time, beating Aston Villa 3–0.

1892 – Darwen are beaten 12–0 in Division One – a top-flight record that still stands today.

1895 – A third FA Cup final meeting between Albion and the Villa – this time the 'Seals' score after just 39 seconds to win the game 1–0.

1900 – West Bromwich Albion Football Club move to their new home, The Hawthorns. The first game sees Albion draw 1–1 with Derby County in front of a crowd in excess of 20,000.

1901 – The Baggies are relegated to Division Two for the first time.

1902 – Albion make an instant return to Division One winning promotion at the first time of asking.

1912 – The Baggies reach a record sixth FA Cup final, but after drawing the first game with Barnsley 0–0, the Tykes triumph 1–0 in the replay.

1920 – Despite losing 10 games during the 1919/20 campaign, Albion are crowned League champions for the first and, to date, only time after winning 28 of their 42 games.

1931 – Albion's record as England's finest cup side continues with a 2–1 win over the Blues in their seventh FA Cup final. It was Albion's first visit to Wembley Stadium and they set a unique record of winning promotion from Division Two during the same season – a double yet to be emulated.

1935 – An EIGHTH FA Cup final ends in a sixth loss, this time to Sheffield Wednesday by a score of 4–2.

1937 – The FA Cup tie with Arsenal sets a crowd record at The Hawthorns with 64,815 people watching a match the Baggies win 3–1.

1954 – One of the greatest ever Albion sides almost write their names into history – but not quite! Nine straight League wins from the off see the title go down to the wire but a 1–0 home defeat to Wolves sees the League title go back to Molineux. FA Cup final number 9 sees Albion beat Preston North End 3–2 to at least win the competition for a third time.

1966 – Albion's tenth major domestic final sees a League Cup final with West Ham played over two legs. The Hammers win the first leg 2–1, but the Baggies romp home 4–1 in the return leg at The Hawthorns to lift the trophy at the first attempt.

1966 – Albion's League Cup triumph ensures a first qualification for the Fairs Cup (now the Europa League) but Bologna ensure the Baggies fans' dreams of glory are shattered with a 6–1 aggregate win in the third round.

1967 – Albion reach a second successive League Cup final against Third Division QPR, but despite West Brom starting red-hot favourites, the Hoops, inspired by Rodney Marsh, roar back from behind to win 3–2 at Wembley.

1968 – England's most prolific FA Cup side reaches its eleventh final and Jeff Astle's solitary strike beats Everton 1–0 to bring the trophy back to The Hawthorns for the fourth time. Astle also writes his name into the record books by scoring in every round.

1969 – Albion go out in the FA Cup semi-final as they attempt to defend their title.

1970 – The Baggies' fourth League Cup final in four years ends in defeat to Manchester City, despite Jeff Astle's early goal.

1978 – Another FA Cup semi-final appearance but Ipswich Town emerge victorious and go onto win the trophy.

1979 – Albion's 'golden generation' of players finish third in the top division after a magnificent campaign.

1981 – Another terrific League campaign sees the Baggies finish in fourth position.

1982 – The end of Albion's halcyon days with another 'so near, so far away' campaign that sees them reach the FA Cup and League Cup semi-finals, only to fall at the final hurdles.

1986 – Relegated to the (old) Division Two.

1991 – The Baggies sink to an all-time low with relegation to Division Three for the first time in the club's history.

1992 – After one season down among the dead men, Albion claw their way out of the third tier of English football after beating Port Vale 3–0 at Wembley.

2000 – Albion lose to Bolton Wanderers in the Division One play-off semi-final.

2002 – The Baggies claim a place in the Premiership for the first time after a 16-year absence by winning their final game of the season against Crystal Palace, edging Wolves out of the automatic berths (ha ha!).

2003 – Albion relegated back to Division One after one season among the 'elite'.

2004 – The Baggies promoted back to the Premiership as runners-up to Norwich City.

2005 – A 2–0 win over Portsmouth on the final day completes 'The Great Escape' with the seemingly doomed Baggies somehow avoiding what had appeared to be certain relegation, thanks to a bizarre permutation of results all going the club's way – Crystal Palace, Southampton and Norwich all perish.

2006 – Relegated back to Division One.

2008 – Promoted back to the Premier League.

2009 – Relegated back to the Championship as the yo-yo years continue.

AND FINALLY . . . BIG RONISMS – (BUMPER) VOLUME 4

Here are the last of Mr Atkinson's quotes – all, it has to be said, reproduced with great affection. . . .

'He'll take some pleasure from that, Brian Carey. He and Steve Bull have been having it off all afternoon.'

'His white boots were on fire against Arsenal, and he'll be looking for them to reproduce tonight.'

'When Scholes gets it [tackling] wrong, they come in so late that they arrive yesterday.'

'This is the best Man United have played in Europe this season and, conversely, the opposition has been excellent.'

'There are a few tired limbs in the blue legs.'

'Scholes and Van Nistelrooy drugged the last two defenders.'

'Ryan Giggs is running long up the backside.'

'He could have done a lot better there, but full marks to the lad.'

'Jari Litmanen should be made compulsory.'

'Heskey needs to punch his own weight.'

'Apart from picking the ball out of the net, he hasn't had to make a save.'

'Scholes is very influential for England at international level.'

'At international level, giving the ball away doesn't work too often.'

'You know when I say that things happen in matches? Well, it just happened there.'

'They've certainly grown, the Japanese. I mean grown in stature, playing-wise.'

'Liverpool will think "we could have won this 2–2."'

'I'm sure Bobby won't want them to be losing the match before winning it.'

'Their forward got a lucky squeeze from the defender.'

'Yordi circumnavigated Ledley King there.'

'Lee Dixon will be up against two South American left-handers tonight.'

'Think of a number between 10 and 11.'

'You don't want to be giving away free kicks in the penalty area.'

'How are they defensively, attacking-wise?'

'The ball goes down the keeper's throat where it hits him on the knees to say the least.'

'He should get his head to those. He is twelve foot tall.'

'He had acres of time there.'

'That's not the type of header you want to see your defender make, with his hand.'

'His head just disappeared into his shoulders.'

'They scored too early.'

'Chelsea are the team who can break the Arsenal and Manchester United monopoly.'

'We haven't had a strategic free kick all night. No one's knocked over attackers ad lib.'

'You can see the ball go past them, or the man, but you'll never see both man and ball go past at the same time. So if the ball goes past, the man won't, or if the man goes past he'll take the ball.'

'Van Nistelrooy, predating as usual.'